Photographs by Paul R. Cheesman.
Drawings by Juliana H. Nicolai.

PATHWAYS TO THE PAST

A GUIDE TO THE RUINS OF MESOAMERICA

Paul R. Cheesman
Barbara W. Hutchins

International Standard Book Number
0-88290-236-9

Library of Congress Catalog Card Number
83-83440

Horizon Publishers Catalog and Order Number
2001

Printed and Distributed in the
United States of America
by

Horizon Publishers & Distributors, Inc.

50 South 500 West
P.O. Box 490
Bountiful, Utah 84010

Contents

J. Nicolai '83

Ruins in Southern Mexico
and in the Yucatan Peninsula
Gulf of Mexico
Gulf of Tehuantepec
Caribbean Sea
YUCATAN
QUINTANA ROO
CAMPECHE
MEXICO
GUATEMALA
MEXICO
BELIZE
Ruins
0
25
50
100
N
Tampico
Panuco
Tempoal
Tuxpan
Santiago de la Pena
Poza Rica
EL TAJIN
Gutierrez Zamora
Papantla
Nautla
Pachuca
Teziutlan
Perote
Jalapa
ZEMPOALA
TULA
TEOTIHUACAN
Mexico City
Puebla
Cofre de Perote
Pica de Orizaba
Orizaba
Boca Del Rio
Veracruz
Anton Lizardo
Cordoba
Fortin de las Flores
XOCHICALCO
Cuernavaca
Cuautla
Izucar de Matamoros
Tehuacan
Alvarado
San Andres Tuxtla
Catemaco
LA VENTA
Coatzacoalcos
Juan Diaz Covarrubias
Acayucan
Minatitlan
Jaltipan
Acatlan
Teotitlan del Camino
Huajuapan de Leon
Huizo
Etla
Oaxaca
Azompa
Santa Maria del Tulu
Teotitlan del Valle
MITLA
Mitla
MONTE ALBAN
San Bartolo Coyotepec
Santo Tomas Ocotlan
Tlacolula
Tehuantepec
Juchitan
Salina Cruz
Tapanatepec
Arriaga
Tonala
Puerto Escondido
Puerto Angel
Tapachula
Tuxtla Gutierrez
San Cristobal Las Casas
Comitan
Teapa
Villahermosa
Catazaja
Palenque
PALENQUE
Frontera
San Roman
Zacatal
Ciudad del Carmen
Puerto Real
Isla Del Carmen
EDZNA
Champoton
Chencoyi
Campeche
Cayal
Hopelchen
Escarcega
Xupjil
Chetumal
ALTUN HA
TIKAL
KAMINALJUYU
COPAN
KOBAH
UXMAL
LABNA
SAYIL
Muna
Uman
Merida
Progreso
DZIBULCHALTUN
Chicxulub
Izamal
IZAMAL
Kantunil
Piste
CHICHEN ITZA
Peto
Tizimin
Rio Lagartos
Valladolid
X-Can
COBA
Felipe Carrillo Puerto
Puerto Juarez
Cancun
Isla Mujeres
Isla Cancun
Puerto Morelos
Playa del Carmen
San Miguel
Isla Cozumel
Akumal
XEL-HA PARK
Tulum
TULUM
180
127
105
130
129
140
85
190
95
150
160
125
131
185
195
186
261
184
295
307
200

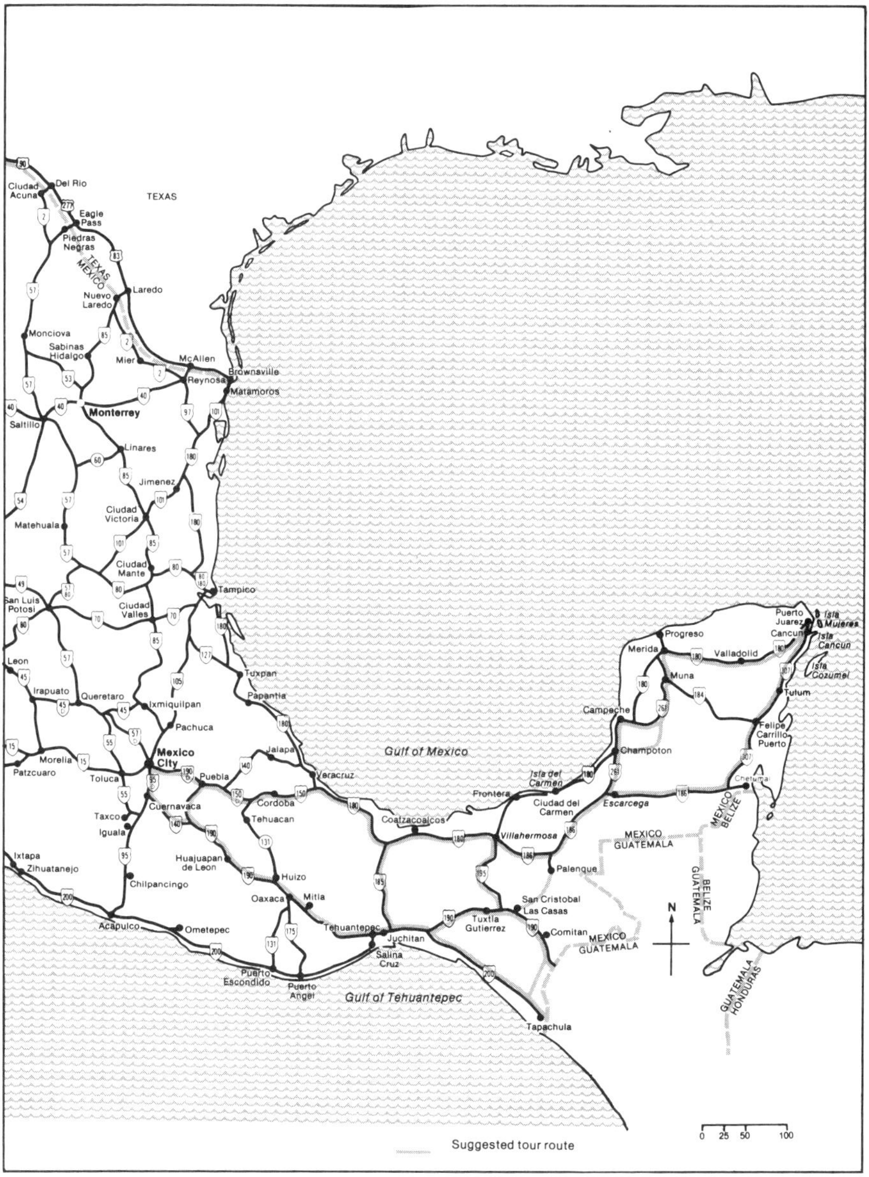

Suggested Routes to Ruins in Southeastern Mexico

Julie Nicolai
'84

List of Illustrations

Introduction

The ancient ruins of once-magnificent civilizations in Mexico, Guatemala, and Honduras have fascinated readers and travelers since they were first discovered by Spanish explorers in the sixteenth century. This interest with its element of mystery has created careers for some and exciting vacations for others. For the novice or the average tourist, however, finding the ruins, knowing the most important facts about them, and about their relationship, if any, to the Book of Mormon have presented challenges hard to overcome.

The authors have spent many years in the study of these civilizations of Ancient America, and many hours and miles traveling to them. Requests have been made of them to make a guide easy to read, understand, and to follow to the great archaeological zones. It is their desire that this book meets these requests.

The purpose of this book, also, is to alleviate the fears of driving to Mexico, lack of knowledge of the Spanish language, and any other apprehensions of travel to a "foreign" country.

This guide to the ancient ruins is not in competition with the many fine guide books that will tell you how to get to Mexico, what to take, and where to stay and eat. It is simply a guide to finding and enjoying the many remnants of civilizations once found in Middle America, and should be used, therefore, as a companion to other books. Hopefully this guide will assist you in determining which of the ruins to visit in the time you have and will help you discover all that is of known importance while you are there. Too often tourists spend anxious hours, or even days, getting to an obscure mark on the map with their only reward the dirt remains from what was removed and taken to a museum. Other times they return home to discover sadly that a very important site alongside a road they traveled was completely overlooked. When you view the sites, you may wonder what they have to do with Book of Mormon times. Do they correlate with the Book of Mormon time periods, legends, cultures, or geography?

If you are a first-time visitor, you will be rewarded and completely occupied with visiting the more publicized and monumental sites. You may easily visit the ancient centers using this guide, or take one of the many fine tours eager to escort you there. Or you may take the trip only in your daydreams. Visiting those sites will give you familiarity with architectural style, building plans and cultural background to fortify your subsequent visits to the less frequented sites.

This book is organized by highway routes so that all the accessible ruins along that road and within an area may be found. The Aztecs inhabited the area around Mexico City and east-central Mexico, the Olmecs were on the coast of the Gulf of Mexico in the area of the Isthmus of Tehuantepec, and the Mayas covered the Yucatan Peninsula, south into Honduras. Since the major ruins and many minor ones are concentrated in these areas, they can be seen in a single trip. The more time you have, obviously, the more you will be able to explore, but even a week is enough time to see the sights in and around Mexico City.

Although this guide will save you hours of wading through volumes of technical material and driving countless wasted miles, you are cautioned that mere visiting without some related reading will provide little real understanding.

Besides being a marvelous vacation, a trip to the ruins in Mexico can inspire study of the Book of Mormon in ways that make the scriptures come alive and be more meaningful. A great family or group project is to see how many clues of the true gospel can be found in the remains of the sites today—Christ, the Tree of Life, resurrection, sacrifice, the priesthood, heaven, hell, the devil, Hebraic signs and facial features, similarities in symbols of Old and New Worlds, and on and on.

In addition to reading the Book of Mormon and historical and geographical books, it is suggested that your visit to the world of ancient America begin and end with the Mexican National Museum of Anthropology in Mexico City—by far the greatest storehouse of pre-Columbian culture in the world.

Come with us on a journey to the past. It doesn't matter if you actually go in body or just in spirit through reading about these fascinating remnants of bygone days.

Cross the border and enter into another world. You will never read the Book of Mormon with complacency again.

CHAPTER ONE

Discovering the Ruins

"Las Ruinas"—"Zona de Arqueologico"—"Los Pyramides"—these are signs seen all over Mexico and her neighboring Mesoamerican countries of Guatemala, Belize, El Salvador, and Honduras.

And these are the signs which lead to mysterious and intriguing cities, temples, pyramids, and ceremonial centers. Remnants of a forgotten past, all these ruins—sometimes stately, sometimes crumbling—are grand evidences of civilizations that lived, flourished, then disappeared, leaving only undecipherable carvings and puzzling god-figures to tantalize modern man.

Explorers and researchers have been amazed by and interested in unlocking the mysteries of the ancient civilizations ever since they were discovered by the New World conquerors. To discover the meaning of these forgotten ruins has inspired lifetime studies by scholars through the years.

To members of The Church of Jesus Christ of Latter-day Saints and students of their Book of Mormon, these ruins have a special meaning.

We know that there were three migrations of people from the Old World to the New World starting sometime around the fall of the Tower of Babel.

But where did they arrive and where did they build the great cities and cultures written of in the Book of Mormon? The book does not say. And God, who inspired the migrations and the writing of the Book of Mormon that tells of their cultural and spiritual experiences, does not say.

Could these people of the Book of Mormon be some of the people who populated Mesoamerica? No one else has any valid answers concerning the identity of these New World inhabitants. There are many evidences, however, that lend to the making of favorable comparisons between the two civilizations.

Early Historians

Even though hundreds of books and papers have been written about the ruins and civilizations in Middle America, the only actual information and knowledge come from just a few sources.

The first people to become acquainted with, and write about, the inhabitants of the New World were the Spanish conquerors. Hernán Cortez and his 400 Spanish soldiers arrived in Veracruz in 1519. Cortez wrote letters back to Spain describing what he found. One of his generals, Bernal Díaz, kept a detailed diary. This was published in book form, entitled *The Discovery of and Conquest of Mexico*, and became very popular in the literary field.

Along with Cortez were Catholic priests who kept records and gradually taught the natives to speak Spanish so they could communicate with each other. Fray Bernardino de Sahagun arrived in Mexico in 1529, eight years after the forces of Cortez conquered Mexico. His first job was to convert the Aztec language into a phonetic alphabet, after which he spent the rest of his life questioning the natives living before and after the Spanish conquest, thus recording their history and culture from the stories he collected. The original manuscript of Sahagun's work was discovered in 1793 in the Laurentian Library in Florence, Italy. It consisted of some 1300 handwritten pages with several watercolor illustrations by an Aztec artist.

Sahagun spent twenty-five or more years gathering this information and he wrote part of the work himself. He also had the Indians write. He edited all of the information at least once, and usually twice. He then asked groups of Indians to recheck his work for accuracy. Finally he collected this into what was to become twelve volumes, written in both Spanish and Aztec.

Sahagun became one of the two great masters of the Nahuatl or Aztec language. He is credited with writing a vocabulary in Aztec, as well as many other writings.

Friar Diego de Landa, a Spanish priest, described the Mayan way of life as he witnessed it. His book *Relación de las Cosas de Yucatán* has been used by researchers as an accurate source of information and has been quoted extensively.

Another chronicler was Fernando de Alva Ixtlilxochitl, the grandson of the last native king of Texcoco, where present-day Mexico City is located. He compiled the *Annals of Ixtlilxochitl*, a historical document written in the sixteenth century that contained the history of his ancestors taken from the legends and stories gathered from his people.

In 1543, the Maya Indians wrote three books from their traditions and ancient documents. The Cakchiquels wrote *The Annals of the Cakchiquels* at Solola, a town overlooking Lake Atitlán in Guatemala. The other two manuscripts, written by Quiche Maya Indians in Guatemala, are *Title of the Lords of Totonicapan*, written at Totonicapan, and the *Popol Vuh*, written at Chichicastenango. The *Popol Vuh* is a collection of traditions and histories written down by one or more Quiche Indians soon after the Spanish conquest.

The next most recent factual books about the ancient ruins were written by John L. Stephens, entitled *Incidents of Travel in Central America, Chiapas and Yucatán*, volumes I and II. Stephens, a lawyer, explorer and writer, and an artist, Frederick Catherwood, made arrangements for a tour of Central America in 1839. At that time all the countries that now comprise Central America were one country. The United States Minister to that country suddenly died, and the President of the United States, Martin Van Buren, appointed Stephens to fill the office since he was going there. The diplomatic appointment was for a specific purpose and did not require a residence at the capital, so Stephens and Catherwood were at liberty to travel. The journey occupied seven or eight months of the years 1839 and 1840.

The books Stephens published became very popular and created a great interest in the ancient ruins so vividly described and illustrated. These books are still used for research and have proved an invaluable source of information about the ruins.

At the same time Stephens and Catherwood were making their journey, the members of The Church of Jesus Christ of Latter-day Saints were being unmercifully persecuted in Missouri. In 1839, Joseph Smith, Prophet and President of the Church, visited President Van Buren, petitioning for assistance needed as a result of these persecutions. Van Buren, fearing election reprisals, denied help, and, in effect, washed his hands of the whole matter.

It seems ironic that this president of the United States, who was considered an enemy to the Mormon people, would unknowingly be the person instrumental in sending Stephens to Central America. Until Stephens's books were published, little was known of the ruins and lost civilizations. His books brought their attention to the world and became the source for further research. These explorations are constantly continuing in these lands, thought by some to be the lands of the Book of Mormon. Regardless of personal opinions about the geography of the Book of Mormon, Stephens's books have greatly assisted the interest in The Church of Jesus Christ of Latter-day Saints.

Ruins of Interest to LDS

The pre-Columbian ruins of Mexico and Guatemala are especially interesting for those familiar with the teachings of the Book of Mormon. For years many researchers in The Church of Jesus Christ of Latter-day Saints have compared the legends of the American Indians, ancient writings of the natives and Spanish conquerors, archaeological findings, distances, topography, time periods, and cultural and religious similarities, and have come to the conclusion that the area of Mesoamerica (southern and eastern Mexico, Belize, and Guatemala) could be the lands written about in the Book of Mormon.

Except for the fact that the immigrants did land somewhere on the American continents, the exact location of the lands of the Book of Mormon has not been revealed. Attempts to pinpoint locations are merely conjecture. However, just as archaeologists in the Near East use the Bible as a guide to search for lost Biblical cities, LDS researchers are using the Book of Mormon to identify where, on the American continents, the lost cities of the Book of Mormon might be located.

Time Periods Compared

The civilizations in the New World were known to be flourishing during the same years mentioned in the Book of Mormon, which leads to interesting correlations of time periods. The first of the three migrations told about in the Book of Mormon was that of the Jaredites who arrived about 2000 B.C., the time of the destruction of the Tower of Babel, which coincides with the rise of a group, in Mesoamerica, known as the Olmecs. The Olmecs are the first of the recorded civilizations of the pre-Columbian cultures. They resided along the Gulf Coast of Mexico near the Isthmus of Tehuantepec.

Other Peoples Represented

There are many indications to show that there were people already on the American continents when the Book of Mormon people arrived from Jerusalem and the Near East, and migrations from other countries are apparent. Facial features in sculptures and other art forms display a variety of styles. "But, said he, notwithstanding our afflictions, we have obtained a land of promise, a land which is choice above all other lands; a land which the Lord God hath covenanted with me should be a land for the inheritance of my seed. Yea, the Lord hath covenanted this land unto me, and to my children forever, and also *all those who should be led out of other countries by the hand of the Lord.* (2 Nephi 1:5; italics added.)

Histories Compared

From 2000 B.C., histories of the Book of Mormon people and pre-Columbian people relate to the rise and fall of various groups and to their high degree of culture and intelligence. The main group of Book of Mormon people left Jerusalem in 600 B.C., by boat. They were led, under divine guidance, by the prophet Lehi and his sons Laman, Lemuel, Nephi, and Sam. After arriving somewhere on the American continents, Laman and Lemuel rebelled against the word of God while Nephi and Sam remained faithful. The two opposing groups soon became known as the Lamanites and the Nephites. Each went their own ways except in times of war or when Nephite prophets tried to convince the Lamanites to return to God and the teachings of Jesus Christ. Sometimes the prophets had great success, but most of the time the more worldly ways of the Lamanites could not be changed. However, by the time a great and final war occurred in the third century A.D., the Nephite culture had declined and they had become as vile as the Lamanites.

The history of the tribes in Mexico runs in a similar way. From the Olmecs several different groups emerged with the Maya the largest, occupying the Yucatán Peninsula south into Guatemala. Tribal conflict and fighting were prevalent among the groups. When a new group conquered an older, more established group, new constructions were often made over the ruins of older ones and the older tribe's cultural and religious customs were adopted. Many legends were perpetuated this way.

Legend of Quetzalcoatl

One of the most uncanny comparisons of stories handed down from people to people through the ages is the legend of a god named Quetzalcoatl compared with the story of Jesus Christ in the Book of Mormon.

The early prophets in the Book of Mormon prophesied of the birth, death, and resurrection of Jesus Christ. It was recorded that, on the night before He was born in Bethlehem, there was no darkness in the New World and a new star appeared and that, when Christ was crucified, there were earthquakes, tempests, fires and whirlwinds, physical upheavals, and darkness for three days. Afterwards, the resurrected Christ came to visit his "other sheep" (John 10:16)—His faithful followers on the American continent. This man, clad in a white robe, descended from heaven and stood in the midst of the people. He dwelt with them, taught them many great and wonderful things, then arose into the heavens again, promising to return in the last days.

Legends of Indian tribes in the Americas tell of the creation, of a great flood, and of ancestors who came from the east (some say at the time of the destruction of the great tower). These tribes knew that a great man—white, bearded and wearing a robe—came to them from the sky, taught them great things, then left in the sky after promising to return.

Because this man "flew" into the sky, he became symbolized as a bird called the "quetzal." The flight of a quetzal bird is serpent-like, in an undulating fashion. Another symbol of this great white deity was the serpent, which is mentioned in the Old and New Testaments as well as in the Book of Mormon (Num. 21; 89; John 3:14-15; Hel. 8:14-15; Alma 33:18-19). The Mexican word for serpent is "coatl." Thus the name of the great white father was "Quetzalcoatl" (kay-sahl-kwa-tl). The combination of the bird and the serpent evolved into the feathered serpent—a symbol found in various art forms throughout Middle America.

Gospel of Jesus Christ Known in Ancient America

From all indications, some of the early inhabitants of the New World had full knowledge of the true gospel as revealed by Jesus Christ. However, with the infiltration of other migrants and their cultures, as well as general apostasy, these "Christian" teachings became extremely distorted and many of them were lost. Remnants of the original religious ideas prevail, though. The belief of the return of the Great White Father, Quetzalcoatl, persisted through the centuries and was so strong when Hernán Cortez and his Spanish conquistadores landed near Veracruz in 1519 that Moctezuma, the ruler of the Aztecs, sent troups to worship him. One of the reasons Moctezuma was convinced Cortez was the awaited god was that, according to the Aztec calendar, Cortez arrived at the place and on the exact day that it was prophesied the deity was to come.

Spanish Catholic priests who accompanied the conquerors into Mexico were astonished to find so many Christian-like beliefs among the natives. Along with these doctrines, however, were idol worship, barbaric human sacrifice, and cannibalism. Because of these depravities, the padres proceeded to destroy all the books and idols they could get their hands on. One priest in particular, Friar Diego de Landa, burned some 5000 idols and 27 hieroglyphic rolls. These rolls were the written records the Mayas kept and only a few remain today. So far no one has been able to read them other then to identify some names and dates. At the end of his life, de Landa wrote a comprehensive history of the Mayas as he found them which has proved to be an invaluable account of the daily lives and culture of the natives in the 1500s.

By the time the Spaniards came, however, the natives of Mexico had deteriorated in culture and achievements. It was hard to realize they were the offspring of the people who had such advanced knowledge in areas like astronomy, who had a system of mathematics equal to any in the world, and a complex system of writing. They were a people who built great cities, erected magnificent pyramids and ceremonial centers and connected them with thousands of miles of roads. After about A.D. 900, the Mayas drifted into obscurity and developed no more. Other groups, including the Aztecs, zoomed to power but their lives were built on barbarianism. Very little is known about the lives of the early people, and their culture remains concealed in a cloud of mystery. All that is left are the ruins of some of their once magnificent temples and cities and art work that defies description. Even though the Mayan language remains with the Mayan people today they, themselves, do not know the secrets of their glorious ancestors.

Mesoamerica and the Land of the Book of Mormon

For several centuries, these mysteries have intrigued people all over the world and the fascination in learning more of the pre-Columbian people in Mexico is as strong as ever, especially among students of the Book of Mormon.

Taking into consideration all the similarities of the histories, oral legends, archaeological evidences, geographical dimensions, and time periods in Mesoamerica and the Book of Mormon, LDS researchers find they compare favorably. Several of them have reached some theoretical geographical conclusions.

These researchers feel that the Isthmus of Tehuantepec could be the "narrow neck of land" dividing Desolation and "the Land Northward" from Bountiful and "the Land Southward." A hill, Cerro Vigia, near the town of Santiago Tuxtla meets all the required criteria for the Hill Cumorah; the Grijalva River could be the River Sidon; the Land of Nephi could be around Guatemala City (Kaminaljuyú); and Zarahemla could be in the state of Chiapas. These are theories formed after years of study and exploration, but until actual locale is divinely revealed, they remain only theories.

CHAPTER TWO

The Civilizations

In order for a traveler to really enjoy his trip, he should learn about the area in which he plans to travel. The history of pre-Columbia Mexico is interesting to read at any time, but is especially so if you plan to visit the country. Knowing the background of the civilizations there enables you to fully appreciate what you see.

Confusion

Hundreds of books have been written by learned scholars about the civilizations that dwelt in Mesoamerica, the land from southern Mexico to Honduras. It is easy to become completely confused by the number of names of cultures, places, dates, facts, etc., that are discussed. For this reason, this book does not attempt to cover all detailed data. One reason for this decision, too, is that so many of the researchers arrive at different conclusions as to dates and history. They admit they do not know where the people originated or how they became so highly cultured. Maybe this work will inspire some readers to investigate more deeply into unraveling the mysteries of ancient American cultures.

The Cultures and Time Periods

Archaeologists usually divide the history of Mesoamerica into four major time periods (as shown on the Time Scale): the Archaic (3000 B.C. and earlier); the Pre-Classic (2000 B.C. to A.D. 300); Classic (A.D. 300 to A.D. 900); and the late or Post-Classic A.D. 900 to A.D. 1520 or the time of the Spanish conquest).

The Classic period refers to the time the civilization was at its peak of development, with Pre-Classic referring to the era of ascension to the peak, and Post-Classic to the time the development was deteriorating.

The Book of Mormon time period was the Mesoamerican Pre-Classic.

TIME SCALE

For the purpose of identifying the ancient cultures of the New World, the writers wish to establish the following periods:

Post-Classic	Late	A.D. 1520
		A.D. 1200
	Early	A.D. 1600
		A.D. 900
Classic	Late	A.D. 900-600
	Early	A.D. 500-300
Pre-Classic	Late	A.D. 300-300 B.C.
	Middle	500-1000 B.C.
	Early	1000-2000 B.C.
Archaic		3000 B.C. and earlier

The times stipulated are approximate, but the major groupings are accepted by qualified authorities in the field. Some experts, however, disagree on the subtitle classifications, and the writers assume the responsibility for the groupings as listed, basing these periods on a comparison of several accepted references.

During these centuries there were numerous cultures of peoples in both North and South America, as well as in Mesoamerica. From Alaska south into Mexico were groups such as Navajo, Hopi, Cherokee, and many more, comprising the North American Indians. In South America the major tribes were concentrated mainly in Ecuador and Peru. These included the most well-known, the Incas, as well as the Chancay, Chavin, Chimu, Mochica and the Nasca.

The major groups in Mesoamerica were the Olmec, Maya, Zapotec, Toltec, Huastec, Mixtec, Totonac, and the Aztec.

In detailed histories of each culture their time periods are broken into the same Pre-Classic, Classic, and Post-Classic periods. More is known of the Olmec, Maya, and Aztec than of the other Mesoamerican groups. The Olmecs were considered to be the "mother culture" and the Aztecs the most recent.

Some of the groups were peaceful; others were warlike. Some would move from one area to another for agricultural reasons, leaving their centers to the elements, while others would attack their neighbors and take possession of the conquered land.

For simplification, this book will discuss only the three most prominent Mesoamerican cultures: Olmec, Maya, and Aztec.

The Olmecs

The oldest (and the strangest) of the native New World civilizations, the Olmecs were virtually unknown to archaeologists until about sixty years ago. Its true importance has only recently been realized. New and exciting research has shown the Olmecs to be the "mother" culture of all the civilizations in Mesoamerica. They were the very first American Indians to achieve a high level of social, cultural and artistic complexity. This level was reached three thousand years ago when David and Solomon ruled in Israel, and when Egypt was in a period of decline. Even though the Olmecs seemed to have a form of writing, there are no reliable documents telling their history. Since historians cannot tell their story, it is up to archaeologists—armed with methods and theories that have largely come to them from the natural sciences and from anthropology—to bring to life this dead and forgotten culture.

There is evidence of the Olmecs' existence by 2000 B.C. and before. However, their culture did not start to expand until around 1500 B.C., with the height of development being around 1200 B.C. This lasted until about 600 B.C., when their culture gradually declined.

The Olmec territory runs parallel to the coast of the Gulf of Mexico and is approximately 120 miles long and 30 miles wide. The most important Olmec centers were La Venta (the best known), Tres Zapotes, and San Lorenzo. These sites are in the state of Veracruz and part of Tabasco, located in a semi-circular area in and just north of the Isthmus of Tehuantepec. (See map p. 35.)

The Olmec Indians evolved a truly incredible culture in an area that would seem to us who dwell in a more temperate region to be almost impossibly hostile. In the very hot, very wet, tropical lowlands of the Mexican states of Veracruz and Tabasco, amid a tangle of rivers, swamps, high jungle, and savannas, they built their great temple centers and carved huge stone monuments. These were the conditions in which the New World's first civilization arose. How and why these people did what they did are perplexing questions to researchers today. If these questions could be answered, it might give a clue as to how the tropics could be used to best advantage for people today.

The name "Olmec" means "people of the land that produces rubber," and was given to them by the Aztecs. The group the Aztecs knew were a later culture, but for the sake of convenience, the name "Olmec" is used for the older generation, too. It is an inaccurate and misleading name for the great early culture of southern Veracruz and Tabasco, but even though attempts have been made to change it to something more fitting, that name has stuck.

The Olmecs were known for their ball game played with a solid rubber ball in a formal court. The game was both a ceremonial event and a form of recreation throughout Mesoamerica. There are pre-Columbian ball courts in Arizona, also. It is suggested that the game was played by two opposing teams bouncing a rubber ball on their hips or elbows. The ball had to go through a stone circle on each side of the I-shaped court. Losers often met death on a sacrificial altar. Ball courts can be seen at Chichén Itzá, Monte Albán, and at many other ancient sites.

The Olmecs are probably best known for the enormous stone human heads found in their area. Since the heads wear helmets, some say they are representative of ball players; others say they are chiefs or kings, but no one knows for sure. Most puzzling, they have thick lips and noses, and Oriental eyes. Made of volcanic rock, the stone heads weigh up to 20 tons, and are all of one piece. A total of twelve have been found so far.

Two of the heads were found in Tres Zapotes, five in San Lorenzo, four in La Venta, and another was recently located near the town of Santiago Tuxtla. Since there are no stone quarries in the area, it is believed that the stone heads and other monoliths weighing more than 50 tons were brought from quarries in San Martin Pajapan, Veracruz, about 78 miles away. The manner in which these enormous monoliths were transported in Olmec times remains a mystery, although it is suggested that they were placed on rafts which were moved by means of rollers.

Oil has been discovered in this Gulf of Mexico shoreline, so the heads and the monoliths have been taken out for preservation. Most of the stone heads have been placed in museums (one can be seen in the Museum of Anthropology in Mexico City), but the majority of the artistically carved monoliths can be found in the outdoor Museum of La Venta at Villahermosa, Mexico.

Influence of the Olmecs has been found all over Mesoamerica, from Teotihuacán (the pyramids north of Mexico City), Monte Albán (near Oaxaca), to Kaminaljuyú (Guatemala City). The fact that the Olmecs were the origin of almost all the other cultures in Mesoamerica was determined in 1939 by Matthew W. Stirling in Tres Zapotes. His excavations produced a broken stele (a flat, carved or inscribed stone of rectangular shape) that had been set upright in ancient times behind a flat stone altar typical of the stele-altar complexes found in Classic Maya centers. The stele had an inscription on one face, and an Olmec-like jaguar mask on the other. Stirling immediately recognized the inscription as a date in the Long Count system of dating used by the Classic Maya. The date on the stele correlated with the modern equivalent of a day in the year 31 B.C. This was some 330 years older than the beginning of the Classic Maya civilization (A.D. 300 to A.D. 900). Here was an Olmec-appearing monument with an inscription in what was thought to have been the Maya system, and found far west of the Maya area itself.

The ruins of Izapa by the Guatemala border also indicate the Olmec ancestry to the Maya. The Izapan culture was the bridge between Olmec and Maya. Hieroglyphic writings on stelae as well as methods of recording dates were found at Izapa. The Maya continued their use of the counting system along with the ball game, the supreme importance of jade, the use of red pigments with jade, ceremonial blood-letting, and many items of ritual paraphernalia.

Some Olmeca art is easily recognizable by the baby-faced sculpture, usually with Oriental eyes. One of the best pieces of art is a statue called "The Wrestler." A large collection of art from this area can be seen in the Olmec Hall at the Mexican National Museum of Anthropology at Mexico City.

Since there are strong similarities between Olmec and Jaredite cultures, many LDS researchers believe they could be the same.

The Maya

Because the remnants of this once great civilization were present when the Spanish conquerors arrived, and because they are still present today, much more is known about the Maya culture than is known about other vanished cultures. Covering the largest area of any group, their territory comprised almost half of the state of Chiapas, a little more than half of the state of Tabasco, and all of the states of Campeche, Yucatán, and Quintana Roo in Mexico. The Maya civilization also included the countries of Guatemala, Belize, and parts of El Salvador and Honduras.

Pottery sherds found in Cuello, Belize, show a dating of c. 2600 B.C., so the area was inhabited at least by that time. The height of the Maya civilization, what is known as Classic Maya, was A.D. 300 to A.D. 900 (some place the beginning at A.D. 200). During this time the people constructed magnificent temples, artistically carved stelae, developed the 365-day calendar, knew astronomy, and in general were one of the most highly cultured civilizations the world has ever known. For unknown reasons, however, after A.D. 900, they stopped construction, and left their cities. Gradually their culture deteriorated. By the time the Spanish conquered the Maya in 1540, they were only a shadow of their former ancestors. Much of what is known about them comes from the chronicle written by Spanish Friar Diego de Landa.

The Maya were the first people to develop the use of the zero in counting systems. Their method of counting can be seen on stelae at the various ruins. The zero was usually designated by a stylized shell, a dot for numbers up to five (a dot for each number) and a bar for five. Thus the number 13 would be written with three dots over two bars.

MAYA NUMERICAL NOTATIONS

One of the methods the ancient Maya used in numerical notations was the bar-and-dot system. The dot (•) has a numerical valuation of 5. By varying combinations of these two symbols, the numbers from 1 to 19 could be written. The numbers above 19 were indicated by their positions.

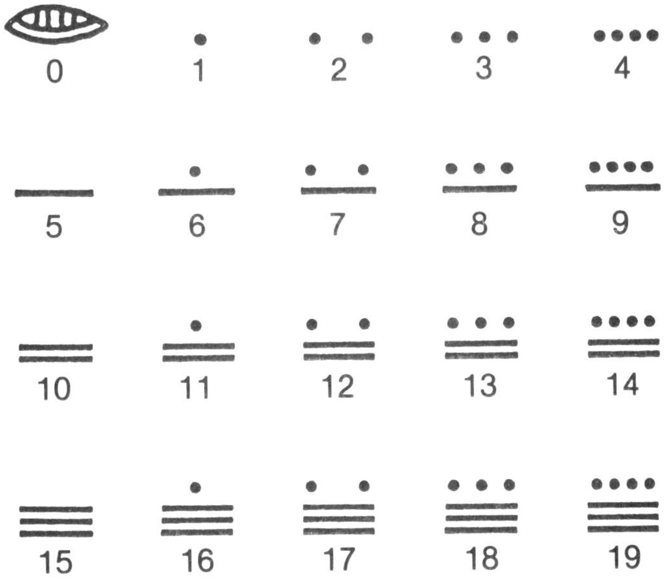

Glyphs for 0 and the numbers 1 to 19 inclusive

Simpler than Roman notation, the Maya bar-and-dot system was superior in two respects. In writing the numbers 1 to 19 in Roman notation it is necessary to use the symbols I, V, and X and the processes of addition and subtraction: VI is V plus I, but IV is V minus I. In order to write the same numbers in Maya bar-and-dot, only the dot and bar are necessary and one arithmetical process of addition.

Artistically drawn blocks called glyphs were used for the ritual almanac days, numbers, solar-year months and other forms of counting. They can be seen on the stele at the ruins.

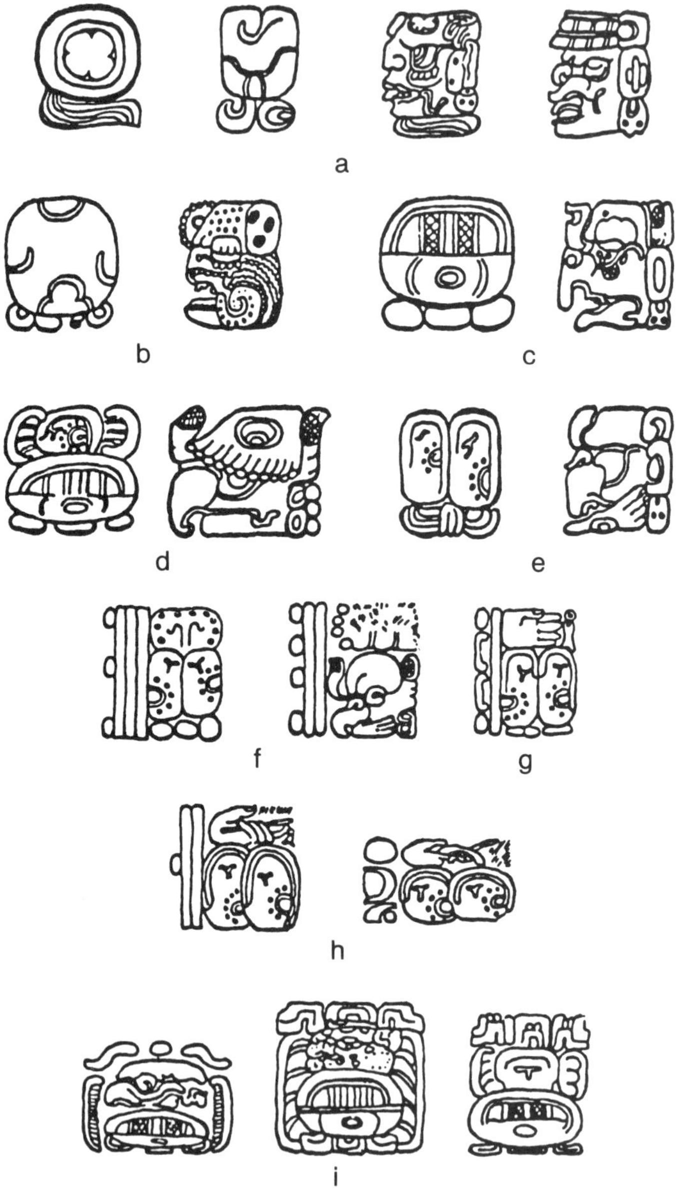

Glyphs for the nine known Maya time periods: (a) kin; (b) uinal; (c) tun; (d) katun; (e) baktun; (f) pictun; (g) calabtun; (h) kinchiltun; (i) alautun.

Today the approximately two million Mayas live just as their progenitors did. No one knows what the original Mayan language was, but it is compared to Latin in that it (Latin) is the mother tongue of the Romance languages. Mayans speak some 24 highland and lowland languages, which are related about as closely as are the various Romance tongues. They have succeeded in preserving their own dialects in spite of four centuries of Spanish domination. Everyday affairs in Mayaland today are conducted in their native language rather than in Spanish.

The Maya are active, energetic, and hardworking, but show little inclination toward leadership or accepting responsibility. Historically, the average man has been a farmer, or in the peasant-artisan class. They were the ones who built the temples and pyramids under the direction of the nobility and priesthood. This work was done to pay a labor tax in exchange for protection from government.

To be competitive is not one of their characteristics. They are content to be small corn farmers, raising just enough food to feed their families and a little more for trading purposes. Some might accumulate a few domestic animals or even become small store owners, but not many go beyond this.

Their diet is extremely low in protein, with the majority of their meals consisting of tortillas and drinks made from maize (corn). Corn was the mainstay of diet—and still is—in all Mesoamerica. Life, cities, and religion centered around its availability and cultivation.

The Maya are scrupulously clean about their person with almost everyone bathing at least once a day. Even though they have to carry their water from the nearest well, they are fanatical about personal cleanliness. The women's dresses, called "huipiles," are brilliantly white with colorful ornamental embroidery. It is amazing how they, and other women all over Mexico, can get their clothes so white since they have to wash them in a tub or in a river by hand.

Their houses are not quite so clean, however. Just as their forefathers did, they live in a "palapa,"—a stick house with a high grass roof. The woman cleans it daily and sweeps the dirt in front, but chickens, turkeys, dogs, goats, and pigs roam at will. Their yards are neatly outlined with rocks. In this small house the children live in a large room with their parents in close contact with the realities of birth, death, and life. The grandparents are expected to provide the moral fiber of the children, and hard work starts when children are ten years old.

In many areas, especially in the jungle away from civilization, the mortality rate among children under age five is very high. The

Washing clothes in Mesoamerica.

Maya have a high birth rate, with the average mother bearing eight children, but she will be able to raise fewer than half of them.

When the Spaniards came in to conquer the Mayas, it was the ruling class who suffered most. The new conquerors took the places of the old civil and religious authorities. Even the priesthood and religion of the Mayas was almost stripped from them to be replaced by Catholic clergy and new icons.

However, what has happened in most instances is that the Mayan "curanderos," or witch doctors, practice their pagan religion comfortably right alongside the priests in the Catholic Church. Since there are many similarities between the old Maya religion and Christianity, the Mayas had no trouble adopting the white man's beliefs. The Maya who lives out of the corrupting influence of the cities lives a life that has been virtually frozen in time. With the beliefs of his ancestors dove-tailing so comfortably with the Christian doctrine, he has been able to continue his religion-family-work-centered life style.

Since the height of Maya development (A.D. 300-900) coincides with the fall of the Nephites, it has been suggested by LDS researchers that the Maya could be the Lamanite remnants left after the last battle at Cumorah.

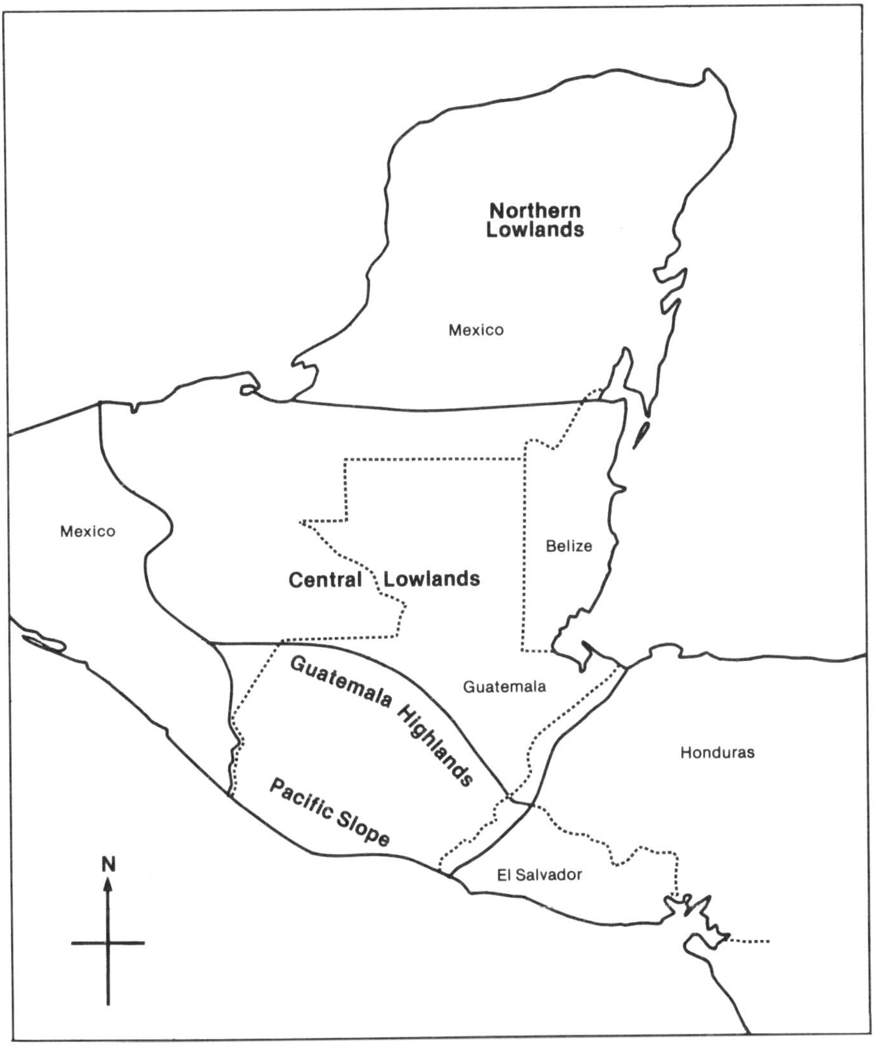

Maya Area

The Nephites taught the doctrines of Jesus Christ for approximately 600 years before Christ's visit to the American continent. After his visit, there were 200 years of peace and prosperity. Gradually apostasy began to set in among the righteous Nephites, and they began to adopt Lamanite customs and ideals. By the time of the great and final war ending in A.D. 421, evil prevailed, and much of the true religion was lost. This degeneration is very apparent in the Maya religion with its gruesome gods and grotesque idols, human sacrifice, and degenerate priesthood. The majority of Mayan people were peace-loving and were content to farm and raise families, but their rulers gained power by insisting that the people appease their gods with gifts and sacrifices. It was these rulers who were the intellectuals who developed the high degree of knowledge.

The Aztecs

In A.D. 900 the Toltecs emerged from the city of Teotihuancán (north of present-day Mexico City) in the Valley of Mexico after its cultural collapse. Political upheaval forced them to move their center to Tula (north of Teotihuacán), where they reached a high cultural level and were outstanding in the arts and sciences. They used the knowledge of other cultures, especially that of the descendants of the Teotihuacán artists who had settled in nearby areas, to augment their own thinking. They also adopted the worship of Quetzalcoatl, a practice which was inherited from previous cultures. The Toltecs flourished for about 300 years. Many of the Toltecs followed their leader Ce Acatl Topiltzin (also known as Quetzalcoatl) to Chichén Itzá on the Yucatán Peninsula.

Soon after A.D. 1300, the Aztecs, a small nomadic tribe, arrived in the Valley of Mexico. It is theorized that they were one of seven Nahua tribes, the Chichimecs, from the northwestern part of Mexico (some sources believe it was the southwestern United States). The place of origin of these tribes was Chicomoztoc, the "place of the Seven Caves." For some, Chicomoztoc is considered to be an actual site. However, for others, it is a mythological and allegorical place, supposedly situated in the northwestern part of Mexico in Aztlan (the land of herons and of whiteness), a place that has never been actually located.

According to recent theories, the Aztecs were separated from the other tribes and arrived in the Valley of Mexico later, settling first near Tula. Meanwhile they had changed their name to "Mexicas" (Meh-shee-kas). Apparently a natural disaster destroyed their town, and they were forced to move.

After several bloody struggles with neighbors, they finally arrived at a small island in the center of Lake Texcoco. According to legend, they were led by their god, Huitzilopochtli. It was here they saw an eagle devouring a serpent on top of a nopal cactus. According to Aztec mythology, this was a sign for them to establish their city there. Today, the Mexican flag has this symbol.

They developed the magnificent city of Tenochtitlán (tay-noch-tee-tlahn), which is now Mexico City, in A.D. 1345.

The Aztec people were, paradoxically, both deeply religious and fervently warlike. They audaciously used intrigue to lure their neighbors into combat, provoking wars in which they acted as mercenaries and extracted profits so that in each conflict they always came out ahead, gaining some piece of land or some other political advantage. Seeing that they were firmly established in their territory, the Aztec rulers attempted to extend their dominion, never ceasing to wage wars of conquest. To succeed in these conquests, they made use of roving traders who served as spies. These spies were taught well to observe and report the organization, customs, economy, and military power of each neighboring town so that later, when the Aztecs thought it was convenient, they could attack them.

Reconstruction of the city of Tenochtitlán as seen at the Mexican National Museum of Anthropology, Mexico City.

No one knows why this nomadic, crude tribe should now unite to be such a powerful force. At first few of the local tribes paid attention to them. They had settled in a marshy swamp no one wanted, and seemed to be "nobody." However, the Aztecs soon learned many of the skills of civilization of those around them. They adopted their neighbors' cultures and incorporated some of their religious beliefs into their own. They benefited from the culture of the earlier Toltecs who lived in the region before them, from the advanced civilization of the Maya of Yucatán, and from the Texcocans whose capital city of Texcoco was on the opposite side of the lake. Texcocans had absorbed the culture of the Toltecas who had absorbed the Teotihuacanos.

Many of their military victories were undertaken to satisfy their religious beliefs. The Aztecs practiced human sacrifice which involved opening the chest of the victim in order to tear out the beating heart. The heart was then offered to their gods. In order to obtain victims for the sacrifices when they ran out of real war prisoners, the Aztecs organized simulated battles with the friendly neighbors, and used these mock prisoners as sacrificial victims. They practiced human sacrifice because they thought it was necessary to feed the sun and their gods with human blood.

They conquered neighboring villages not only for these sacrifices, but for the taxes they could impose on frightened people. No other groups in Mesoamerica were as organized as the Aztecs. By this time they were building their great city of Tenochtitlán, and they hoarded the gold, jade, gemstones and other riches forced from the other tribes.

This practice of subjugation proved to be fatal to the Aztecs and their ruler, Moctezuma.

The Spanish Conquest

On Good Friday, 1519, Hernán Cortez and his troops set foot on land near Veracruz. They had heard of the wonders of the New World, and had come to explore it for the king of Spain and to bring Christianity to the heathens.

When the conquerors arrived in "New Spain," they encountered Indians who tried to fight them off. Even though the natives were numerous they were no match for the guns and horses of Cortez. The Indians thought that the horse and its rider were all one animal, for they had never seen horses before.

From their landing site the soldiers marched to Zempoala, a Totonac capitol of 30,000 situated on the coast of the Gulf of Mexico, near Veracruz. The conquerors easily subdued the Indians, and the Totonacs were soon persuaded to assist Cortez and his men to conquer Moctezuma and the Aztecs. The tribe had recently been subjugated by the Aztecs, so they were willing to fight their oppressors.

It did not take long for Moctezuma to hear of Cortez's landing. Actually, he was looking for the man to come.

> By tradition the return of Quetzalcoatl was predicted for One Reed year (according to the Aztec calendar), and the landing of Cortez at Veracruz in such a year constituted a precise fulfillment, with amazing fidelity, of an ancient prophecy. Such an event had been foretold by the Aztec priests. According to their divinations the returning 'Fair God' would be white-skinned, would have a black beard and would be garbed in black. Had not Quetzalcoatl, before embarking for the 'Land of the Sun' assured his handful of faithful followers that he would return to reestablish his rule in a One Reed year? It would be, he had warned, a 'time of tribulation for the people.' (Reed, *The Ancient Past of Mexico*, p. 47, 1966.)

Moctezuma sent ambassadors to Cortez, acknowledging that the white man was the expected god. He sent precious gifts and vowed allegiance.

When the conquerors saw the gold and jewels, their greed pushed them further inland. During the time they were conquering the natives, the soldiers were telling them they were doing so in the name of Christianity. They would tear down the Indian idols on the temples and in their places put the cross or statues of the Virgin Mary. The people were instructed to worship these icons. Throughout their march into Mexico, the Spaniards would fight and conquer the various Indian tribes along the route from Veracruz to Tenochtitlán, then the Indians would give precious gifts to appease the white men. As Cortez drew nearer to Tenochtitlán, Moctezuma kept sending emissaries with more fabulous gifts to the "white god." The Spaniards were in constant danger, not only in battle, but of being captured and becoming victims of human sacrifices, but only a few met this fate.

In the relatively short period of 200 years this unlikely group of barbarians, the Aztecs, had converted a marshy island of modest proportions into America's largest and most grandiose city. Tenochtitlán, the city of the tenochtli (cactus), or of the followers of the priest Tenoch, gave such an impression that Bernal Díaz, one of Cortez's men, recalled it vividly fifty years after the city's total destruction. Through his writing it is possible to go back in time and gaze at those "wonderful sights" witnessed by the Spaniards as they marched two miles from the mainland to the magnificent twenty-square-mile city reached by a causeway "eight paces in width" and completely crowded with curious people.

Housed in the sumptuous palace of Moctezuma's father in the center of the beautiful city, and with complete freedom of movement, the Spaniards had an opportunity to observe, as no outsider had before (and no one will again), life in Anahuac. They witnessed things even forbidden to the local inhabitants, such as the dining of the great king who was served over 300 plates of exquisite food on Cholula earthenware at a table complete with cloth and napkins. Maids gave him water and towels for his hands, and he drank from pure gold vessels.

Outside the palaces, the city stood gleaming white, as if made of silver, against the tropical blue sky and sparkling lake. The distant horizon was dotted with the surrounding neighboring villages and backed by forest-covered hills and the snow-covered peaks of two cloud-piercing volcanoes.

The immaculate streets of the city ran parallel to the Venice-like boat-filled canals used as transportation for the great amount of traffic. Houses of the lower class were nearer the water and made of light cane and thatch. Those of the wealthy lords of the land were close to the center of the city and constructed of stone and mortar. Most were one-story, but the principle homes were of two-stories with inner patios and profuse flower gardens. In addition to the homes there were many temples and oratories, parks, gardens and groves, and sweet-smelling trees along the brick-lined foot paths which ran parallel to the canals crossed at intervals by wooden bridges. This great city boasted complete armories, voluminous libraries, aviaries, a type of zoo, herb gardens, water fountains and baths, and an aqueduct bringing sweet water into the city from Chapultepec. There were districts for craftsmen working in gold, leather, feathers, and stone. Workers were busy as painters, gardeners, sculptors, weavers, dancers, acrobats, stonecutters, carpenters, masons, and vendors. Indeed, so numerous and unlimited were the sights that Diaz reports the Spaniards could not tire of seeing all the marvels.

The Aztecs spoke the Nahuatl (Nah-wah-t'l) language. Words that end in "tl" are from this language (Quetzalcoatl, etc.). From it came such English words as tomato, chocolate, and chili. Chocolate was a favorite Aztec drink. The Aztec prized it so highly that they used cacao beans for money. Cortez sent chocolate back to Spain, and the drink soon became the rage of all Europe.

It soon became apparent to the Aztecs that Cortez was no Quetzalcoatl. The Spaniards conquered their hosts and Moctezuma was killed. From then on, the course of history for Mexico, the rest of Mesoamerica, and for the ancient civilizations there, was in the hands of Spain.

Since the Aztec civilization existed about one thousand years after the Book of Mormon time period, it is obvious that the Aztecs had nothing to do with the Book of Mormon times or people. However, the Aztecs could have been descendants of these people.

It is known that the Aztecs were great copiers. They adopted their language from numerous other tribes; they took the calendar which had been known to the Mayas under the name of Tzolkin for 1500 years, and they absorbed the religious themes (including the Fair God, Quetzalcoatl) handed down from one generation to another throughout all Mesoamerica. Some of these religious themes are hardly recognizable as coming from the original source, but the fact that they are there would seem to sustain the teachings of Jesus Christ in the Book of Mormon.

EARLY AMERICAN CIVILIZATIONS

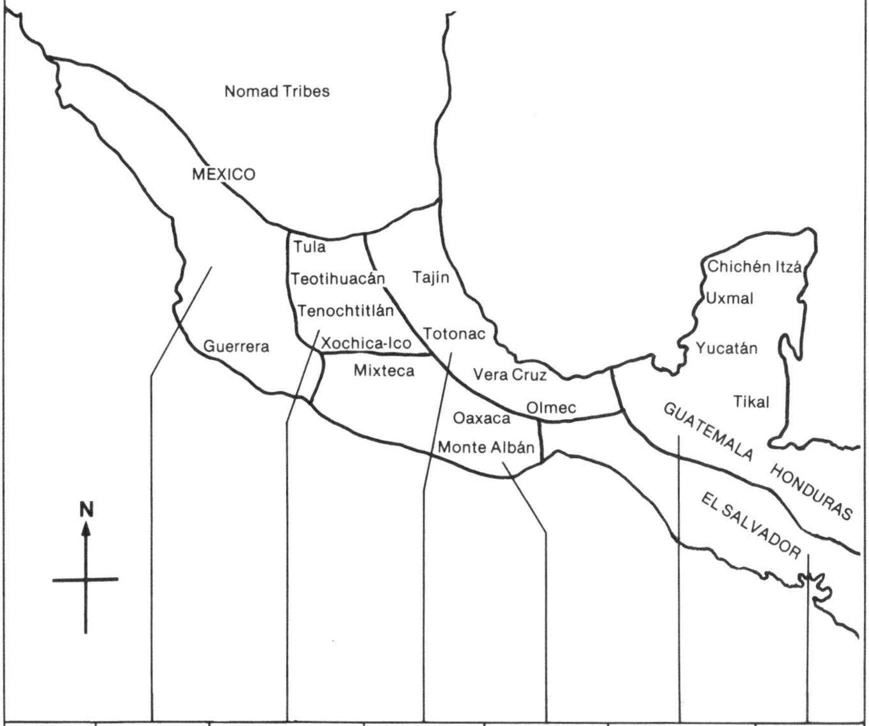

	Occident	Central Mesa	Gulf Coast	Oaxaca	Maya	Pacific
Post-Classic 900 A.D.		Aztec Tula		Mixteca	Chichén Itzá Uxmal	Zaculeu
Classic 300 A.D.		TEOTIHUACAN Xochicalco	Tajín	MONTE ALBAN		KAMINALJUYU
Pre-Classic 2000 B.C.	Guerrero		Olmec		Tikal	

CHAPTER THREE

The Road and the Ruins

About the Country

Mexico—a country of enchantment and beauty. With mariachi bands, sleepy rural villages, cosmopolitan cities, magnificent cathedrals, and intriguing courtyards hidden behind massive, solemn doors—Mexico has a unique combination of influences from her mother country of Spain and from her close neighbor, the United States. Dry, arid deserts, humid tropical jungles, high, snow-capped mountains, and beach resorts that equal any in the world make up a variety of climate and activities to please anyone and everyone.

Mexico is a land of mystery and intrigue, also, for out of these deserts and jungles arise pyramids, larger and more exquisite than those in Egypt, temples projecting above the jungle treetops or covered by lush vegetation, and majestic ceremonial buildings and stelae, worn with time. All these are grand evidences of civilizations who lived, flourished, then disappeared, leaving only undecipherable carvings and puzzling god-figures to tantalize modern man.

Mexico and her neighboring Mesoamerican countries are a paradise for historians, archaeologists, artists, photographers, and especially for travelers who want to see life in a "foreign" country. However, the most captivating sites in Mexico, by far, are the ruins of these ancient civilizations.

The Ruins and the Book of Mormon

When viewing the existing archaeological ruins in Mesoamerica today and trying to relate them to the Book of Mormon, it must be remembered that many of these edifices and temples were constructed several centuries after Book of Mormon times. However, as is demonstrated by the people of the Far East, later civilizations reflect the cultures of many past centuries.

Early External Evidences Deteriorated

Because of the nature of the terrain, most of the equipment and utensils used in everyday life have deteriorated. Iron and metal have rusted and wood has rotted.

In the southern part of Mesoamerica, as in the Land Southward in the Book of Mormon, wood was plentiful. The Nephites and Lamanites were skilled craftsmen in woodworking. In Mosiah 11, which takes place between 160 and 150 B.C., we learn that: "King Noah built many elegant and spacious buildings; and he ornamented them with fine wood . . . And he also built him a spacious palace, and a throne in the midst thereof, all of which was of fine wood." During the Nephite dominance from 200 B.C. to A.D. 322, virtually all buildings in Bountiful were constructed of wood. The Nephites became so skillful in working with wood that they were capable of making ships and boats that would accommodate large numbers of people, as well as fortresses and walls of wood. Structures of wood would last a short time in the humid atmosphere.

When the Nephites moved out of Bountiful into the Land Northward, there was a scarcity of wood because the Jaredites who had previously occupied the region had stripped off the timber and it had not yet had time to become reforested as of 46 B.C. The Nephites had to learn new skills of working with cement and stone.[1]

The state of Oaxaca in Mexico, which is proposed by Book of Mormon researchers to be the Land Northward, is dry and has a terrain of barren hills.

Stone Construction

Some stone buildings that were constructed during earlier periods were used as foundations for later structures. The Nephite / Lamanite and Mesoamerican civilizations would build up a city, life would flourish for a while, then the city would be abandoned. Later another culture would come in and build on top of the older sites. This process is typical of what is found by archaeologists working throughout the world. (There were seventeen buildings and rebuildings of the wall of Jericho after the early Bronze Age (2300-3000 B.C.), and excavations indicate even more layers of civilizations at Megiddo.[2]

Today, the ruins of Chichén Itzá, Monte Albán, and Uxmal are examples of one or more cultures building on top of existing sites. They are also typical of the religious or government centers where the temples and palaces are constructed of stone but the people's homes were (and are today) stick huts with thatched roofs.

---

[1] See footnotes, page 152.

When the visitor views the grotesque gods and hears the gruesome stories of their religious practices involving human sacrifice, it is difficult to relate these acts to the Nephites with their teachings of love and brotherhood. In the Book of Mormon, though, it is the Lamanites and apostate Nephites who are concerned with building great cities. Faithful Nephites built temples and altars, but they were probably made primarily of wood as mentioned in 2 Nephi 5:15-16 and Helaman 3:9. Their deviation from the true religion resulted in more and more emphasis on riches and power.

Reasons for the Deterioration of Morals

From study and observations, it seems that the use of alcohol and drugs might have played an important part in the deterioration of the civilizations in both the Book of Mormon and Mesoamerican civilizations.

In many instances in the Book of Mormon, drunkenness was the undoing of the people. In Mosiah 22, Ammon and King Limhi and the Nephites were able to escape from the Lamanites because the Lamanites were drunk every night. On other occasions the Nephites were able to defeat the Lamanite armies because the Lamanites were drunk. King Noah ". . . built winepresses and made wine in abundance; therefore he became a winebibber, and also his people." (Mosiah 11:15.)

Consumption of alcohol was a severe problem in Mesoamerica when the Spanish conquerors came, according to Friar Diego de Landa. He relates that every festival (which was usually religious) was ended by heavy drinking. It was part of their religious ceremonies for the lords and priests to drink to intoxication.[3]

According to some stories of the ancient peoples, great stress was laid on the need for communication between men and gods. This demonstrates the enormous importance that was given to revelation. Communication of this kind appeared to be achieved through purification of the heart and mind. Since this purification required fasting and, presumably, mental and emotional disciplines, the process of communicating with deities was believed to be intensified and quickened by the use of drugs distilled from native plants. Grown abundantly throughout Mexico, the maguey cactus was the source of alcohol. The juice, today, distilled as tequilla or fermented to make the poor man's drink—pulque—was widely used by the ancients.

They were also habitual users of tobacco, they used copal resin for its incense, and they used many hallucinogenic plants. Modern pharmacologists and psychologists are now studying the properties of these drugs. Irene Nicholson, an author of Mexican mythology, comments:

> The use and abuse of hallucinogens may provide a clue to the perplexing riddle of the degenerations of the ancient cultures; for it is evident that the religion of Quetzalcoatl, the original one of redemption and mercy, had become almost transformed by the time the Spanish armies arrived in the New World.[4]

Spanish chronicler Sahagun wrote of how the Indians ate and drank vision-inducing drugs, and of how they gathered together to sing and dance for sheer joy. He lists dozens of "divine" plants used by the Indians.

Spanish soldiers were horrified by the mass human sacrifices and superstitions and by adoration of multitudes of gods and goddesses in the New World. Some of these seemed, to the soldiers, to be more like demons.

It seems that a genuine priesthood aware of its responsibilities would have needed to be careful about how they used their pharmacological knowledge. Nicholson further comments that:

> . . . a degenerate priesthood could have very quickly discovered that the drugs gave them power, and would have not discriminated between evil and good. This is a far cry from Quetzalcoatl, who could not bear to hurt any living thing. But if the priests had lost all sense of responsibility, the degeneration is easily explained.[5]

Today the people still appeal to the "witch doctors" (curanderos) right inside the Catholic churches to rid them of the demons of whiskey. This practice can be seen in Indian villages of Chamula, Mexico, and Chichicastenango, Guatemala, among other places.

In spite of degeneration and apostasy, though, strains of the original religious teachings have remained in the legends and lives of the Mesoamericans, and this is what Book of Mormon students look for.

Finding the Ruins

For most tourists to Mexico and other parts of Middle America the problems of where the ruins are located, the most important information about them, and the best route to see them arises. To assist those who actually make the journey as well as those who only read and dream of adventure, a suggested plan of travel is presented here. The plan is for those who wish to drive their own vehicle in Mexico to have a description of each archaeological site presented as well as for those travelers who choose other means of touring the country.

What to See In the Time You Have

The schedules given are very conservative, leaving you time for your own further selections of shopping, sightseeing, and leisure time.

After studying the map, you may decide to take other routes to see ruins of your choice in your allotted time.

As with the roads of Rome, all roads in Mexico lead to Mexico City, and that is where your ruins adventure should begin.

The Way to Mexico City

If you especially want the experience of driving in northern Mexico, then take any border crossing you wish. However, the best way to reach the Yucatán area-or the most direct way to Mexico City—is to leave the U.S. by one of the border towns in south Texas (Del Rio, Laredo, McAllen, or Brownsville). Make your plans to do any night driving in the U.S. Driving after dark in Mexico is not advisable. If your trip is taken in the winter months, remember days are shorter and darkness comes by 6:00 p.m.

The scenery in northern Mexico is not too different from that of Arizona and New Mexico—miles and miles of cactus and desert—so the quicker one can get through them and on to the more interesting area, the better. This is accomplished by using the south Texas border towns rather than crossings in Arizona, New Mexico, or even El Paso.

Northern Mexico.

From Laredo to Mexico City the distance is 750 miles, which will take two days, or fewer, depending on how long and how fast you drive. This route uses Highway 85 out of Laredo to Monterrey, Highway 54 to Saltillo, and Highway 57 out of Saltillo to Mexico City.

It is important for the traveler in Mexico not to be in a hurry. Remember, you are in the land of "mañana." And know ahead about your accommodations for the night and arrive before sundown. No night driving.

One-Week Tour

Day 1 and Day 2	Laredo to Mexico City, including a stop at Tula (can be done on the way back if you prefer)
Day 3	Tour of Mexico City and the Mexican National Museum of Anthropology
Day 4	Pyramid of Teotihuacán, 25 miles northeast
Day 5	Pyramid of Cholula (near Puebla, 75 miles east)
Day 6 and Day 7	Return to Laredo

Ten-Day Tour

Day 1 and Day 2	Laredo to Mexico City. Stop at Tula
Day 3	Tour of Mexico City and the Mexican National Museum of Anthropology
Day 4	Remaining sites in Mexico City
Day 5	Pyramids of Teotihuacán
Day 6	Day's drive (340 miles) to Oaxaca, stopping at Cholula, near Puebla
Day 7	The hilltop ruins of Monte Albán and the intricately carved stone fretwork on the facades of temples at Mitla
Day 8	Return to Mexico City via Cuatla and Cuernavaca (faster road)
Day 9 and Day 10	Return to Laredo

Two-or-More-Week Tour

The trip from Mexico City to the Yucatán Peninsula can be made in two weeks. Three weeks will allow for much more exploration.

Of course, this schedule is very general since no exact timing can be presented because of the variances in vehicles and speed of driving. Some people are much more interested in details than others, so more time at each site is required for them.

Mexico City

One of the most unique cities of the world, Mexico City lies in a mountain-rimmed valley 7,400 feet above sea level. The modern city was built over the destroyed Aztec city, Tenochtitlán, which was on an island surrounded by lagoons. Today the water has dried up and the city is built over the whole area. Old buildings such as the Shrine of Guadalupe were constructed over this unstable ground, and are now sinking gradually.

Driving in Mexico City is not for the faint of heart. Even the most experienced driver may be ready for the men in white jackets after attempting to get around town, especially during the rush hours or on a Saturday night. The best day for driving around the city is Sunday.

Public transportation is very good, and don't be afraid to try the Metro system (subway). When the excavation for the subway was being done, the crew came across some Aztec ruins so it was decided to leave as many as possible. At the Piño Suárez subway station a small, round structure can be seen. Don't miss it. There are three subway lines, all well marked.

Leave your car at the hotel or your recreational vehicle at one of the nice trailer parks, and take tour buses, taxis, or engage the services of an official, government-authorized guide who will take you in his car, or drive yours, where you wish to go. These guides can be reached through your hotel or any travel agency.

More evidences of Aztec ruins were discovered in the center of town and excavations will soon change the face of the area. They are by the Zocolo—the main plaza of the city—but a high fence hides the work.

A commercial guide book can give you explicit details of what to see and do in the city, so this book will deal with the pre-Columbian aspects of the area.

In Mexico City the places pertaining to the pre-Columbian era you will want to see are:

The Mexican National Museum of Anthropology (a must!)
The Plaza of Three Cultures
Cuicuilco
Piño Suárez
Tenayuca
Xochimilco
Cerro De La Estrella (Hill of the Stars)
Santa Cecilia Azcatitlán

Also a must on your list is the Mexico City Temple of The Church of Jesus Christ of Latter-day Saints located on Avenida 520 M.C., Colonia Aragon. It is across the street from the Aragon Zoo and the Aragon Social Security Hospital, near the airport. The architectural design depicts the country's pre-Columbian heritage.

Important archaeological sites near Mexico City are:

Xochicalco, 28 miles south of Cuernavaca
Tula, 80 miles north of Mexico City
The Pyramids of Teotihuacán, 40 miles north of Mexico City
Cholula, 75 miles east of Mexico City

The Mexican National Museum of Anthropology

The most important place to visit in Mexico City is this world-famous museum. A miracle of architecture and museum planning, it is easily identified by the 168-ton figure of Tlaloc, the rain god, standing at the entrance of a tunnel leading to the parking area. The museum is located on the Paseo de la Reforma in Chapultepec Park. Off a central patio, there are halls with exhibits of every culture in the history of Mexico. It starts with the origins and the Pre-Classic period, and includes Teotihuacán, the Toltecs, the Mexica, the cultures of Oaxaca, the Gulf Coast cultures, the Maya, the north of Mexico, and western Mexico. Each one of the ruins in the country has been reconstructed in a model to depict what it looked like in its original form.

Demonic Ceremonial Mask
Mexican National Museum of Anthropology

Huehueteotl, God of Fire
Mexican National Museum of Anthropology

The best treasures from the excavated sites have been brought here for exhibit. The burial tomb in the Palace of Inscriptions at Palenque is reproduced here. Life in Aztec times is depicted in a miniature model village. The Aztec calendar stone is on display, as well as cultural maps, and any information desired on pre-Columbian life and archaeology. This is a must.

English-speaking guides will help you to enjoy this unique museum.

Stone box from Ancient Mexico on display at the Mexican National Museum of Anthropology in Mexico City.

Plaza of Three Cultures, Tlatelolco (Place of the Mounds)

In the center of Mexico City, next to an ancient Spanish church (and the modern Ministry of Foreign Affairs and other present-day high-rise buildings) lies a park-like plaza, the Plaza of Three Cultures. Bright new sidewalks and terraces angle through broken-down and little-restored ruins that barely hint at the marvelous structures and events they were anciently a part of. Once a bitter rival, and second only to the great Tenochtitlán complex in importance, this inauspicious stone pile is now one of the few visible remains of the two magnificent ceremonial centers that were at the heart of the Aztec world.

Tlatelolco, Plaza of Three Cultures, Mexico City.

Here the great king, Moctezuma II, took Cortez's hand, and from the top of the towering temple—visible for two and a half miles—pointed out the vast cities, markets, canals, lakes, and causeways that made up the empire. From this pyramid a small group of captured Spaniards was hurled down the steps, minus their hearts, which were sacrificed to the god of war. One of the kings of Tlatelolco had suffered a similar fate here in 1473 when his city was wrested away by the jealous ruling family of Tenochtitlán, and annexed to that rapidly expanding city. Before that, Tlatelolco had been a settlement on the small, but higher island (thus the "place of the mound") by Chichimecs from Atzcapotzalco who had their own government and ruler. When the neighboring island of Tenochtitlán early in history was divided into quarters, disgruntled Aztec emigrants, unhappy with their land settlement, moved over into Tlatelolco.

A guild of traveling merchants lived here among the great palaces and temples, working their way up the social ladder to fame and wealth. Acting as spies for the emperor, they brought rich commerce from all over so that Tlatelolco's market was unsurpassed. The Spaniards, standing in awe before the great complex of stalls

Market day at Tenochtitlán

and activity, described it as three times larger than that of Salamanca, Spain, with some 60,000 persons coming and going. Today, the dwelling units surrounding this area can house the same number of people.

Tlatelolco was the final burial place of the great Aztec nation, for here the last king, Cuauhtemoc, was defeated in 1521 and his kingdom leveled. To this same plaza the Spanish brought many books of Nahua wisdom and learning from all the libraries of the Aztec domain and, in one of history's great losses, burned them in an attempt to eradicate the pagan element. Thus, at the same time, the empire was left in rubble and the cultural heritage in ashes.

Following the destruction and leveling of the Aztec city, the reconstruction began. At Tlatelolco, the "Spanish Phoenix" arose out of the Aztec ashes, for here the Indian workers lived while they constructed the Spanish capital. First, in 1531, they built a church and monastery over the old marketplace. Then America's first college trained the young sons of the deposed Aztec priests and rulers. One young Spanish scholar, Father Sahagun, along with three of his disciples, resurrected the ancient Nahua mind by questioning the pre-conquest survivors and recording in several volumes their legends, customs and knowledge.

Cuicuilco (Kwee-KWEEL-ko)

The ancient town has been covered by lava flow from the eruption of the volcano Xitle (Sheet-lay) which happened about A.D. 34, according to Dr. Bruce Warren of Brigham Young University. The site is a mile south of the University of Mexico City, a short distance north of the quaint area of Tlalpan by way of Avenida Insurgentes. (It can be reached only from the northbound lanes on Insurgentes.)

Lava flow over the town of Cuicuilco, in Mexico City

This is an important ruin because of its age. When the devastation occurred, it left the huge adobe and rock structure standing like an island in a sea of hardened lava. This material now forms the foundation for the buildings of the nearby university. Authorities agree on one thing: this is one of the oldest stone structures standing on the American continent. Certainly it is the oldest in the Valley of Mexico. The time period of this city correlates with that of the

Book of Mormon, indicating both peoples were enjoying a high degree of civilization at the same time.

It is not known exactly when the pyramid was begun, but it was built in various stages over an ancient adobe structure that was rebuilt several times until it finally reached a diameter of 445 feet at the base. Four, and possibly five, circular platforms looking like truncated cones were superimposed on one another. These were topped by rectangular altars or adoratorios made of wood and thatching. Excavations have revealed altars that exist on the third and fourth levels. Access to the top altar was by way of a ramp on the west side and a stairway on the east side. The 65-foot-high structure remaining today was probably closer to 100 feet high at its peak. Some 25 feet of the facing stone were blasted away by archaeologists in recent times to clear off the lava.

Not as spectacular now as it was in former times, the pyramid is still noteworthy on several accounts. Apart from being so ancient, this concept of a man-made hill probably fashioned after one of Mexico's 1500 volcanoes (some have associated this with the tower of Babel concept) and topped by a ceremonial temple, marks the beginning of significant religious architecture in the valley. No doubt this is the forerunner of the magnificent pyramids at Teotihuacán and the Maya area. A large labor force was required to build it, and that may indicate another of Cuicuilco's contributions, for to form labor forces takes highly organized minds. Here we see, also, the beginnings of urbanism and the city-state in Central Mexico. Cuicuilco was undoubtedly the dominating center of the Valley of Mexico during the late Pre-Classic period (300 B.C. to A.D. 300), and, as such, must have contributed to the rapidly growing Teotihuacán whose strength and influence eventually rivaled and then overshadowed Cuicuilco by about A.D. 150.

Surrounding the pyramid in a radial pattern are many simple graves. Other structures surrounded the pyramid also, among them a strange, circular one to the southwest formed of large, inclined stone slabs supporting a stone roof. A serpent was painted on the slabs, in red, now faint. Several altars, including a circular one predating the pyramid, were dug up to the east and west. Small pyramids at nearby Villa Olympica—and undoubtedly more under the lava—attest to the extensiveness of this Pre-Classic ceremonial site.

Near the circular pyramid is a small museum containing ceramic pieces from Cuicuilco and other Pre-Classic sites in the area. Among the artifacts is a statue of the fire-god so prevalent in later cultures. The museum is open daily, except Monday, from 9-5 p.m.

Piño Suárez

One of the fascinating sights to see in Mexico's Metro (subway) Piño Suárez station is the round Aztec pyramid. As mentioned earlier, when the subway construction began in the late 1960s, archaeologists retrieved artifacts and recorded important finds that could not be saved. Remembrances of Spanish soldiers (swords, stirrups, and horseshoes) and household items of every description were found about six feet underground. Farther down, sinking unevenly in the watery subsoil, were the remains of the ancient Aztec city—thousands and thousands of pottery and stone items, portions of temples and other buildings, sections of aqueducts, and the stairway leading to Moctezuma's palace. As subway construction has moved outward toward the suburbs, numerous other archaeological sites have been uncovered. The circular pyramid that was restored and incorporated into the Piño Suárez station (located directly south of the main plaza) was an altar within an immense religious sanctuary that once stretched a quarter of a mile in either direction.

Riding the subway is not necessary to see this pyramid. When you find the station, go down the stairs to see this Aztec ruin.

Tenayuca

This post-Book of Mormon zone is located north of town, before reaching Santa Cecilia where another small pyramid is located. The roads may be under construction, so a recent map would indicate the best directions. The grounds are open from 8 a.m. to 5 p.m. daily.

The pyramid was constructed by the Chichimecs, the cousins of the Aztecs who came from the same area and who belonged to the same language group. It must have been of importance to the Aztecs, for they copied the pyramid style on a much larger scale for their greater pyramids at Tenochtitlán and Tlatelolco. Since the Aztec pyramids are now gone, we can only know them through the remains of the Tenayuca pyramid. All these structures consisted of a single base with a double stairway leading up to twin temples to Tlaloc, the rain god, on the left as you faced the temples, and to Huitzilopochtli, the war god, on the right. The present pyramid-platform at Tenayuca covers an acre of ground, and the original wooden temples burned by Cortez probably stood another 30 feet above the 70-foot-high platform. It is positioned as a dedication to the setting sun on May 19 and July 26.

Perhaps better than any pyramid in Mexico, this one depicts the custom of covering an existing structure to create a greater foundation for a larger temple. Here one can see eight major building stages, begun by the Chichimeca in 1300, and terminated under

Aztec influence. Except for the stairway, the building you see today is what remains from removing the final building stage during reconstruction.

Tenayuca

Two theories are advanced for the superimpositions: either each successive ruler required a more impressive structure, or the building was enlarged following each 52-calendar-year cycle. This cycle was equivalent to our century and was honored to appease the deities. Periodic remodeling can also be seen at Cholula and Teotihuacán.

Especially fascinating at Tenayuca is the wall of 138 serpents (Coatepantli) surrounding three sides of the base of the pyramid. These were originally stuccoed and painted red, black and green; colors of the regions of the universe. Originally about 800 serpent heads probably protruded from the sides of the pyramid, as they did also from other Aztec pyramids. Some other features of the Tenayuca pyramid are:

1. A sepulcher to the right of the pyramid adorned with skulls and bones. Perhaps the tomb into which the sun has fallen in sacrificial death.

2. Two fire serpents on either side probably functioned to guide the setting (dying) sun on its journey through the underworld.

3. Small museum showing a model of the various stages of the pyramid growth. Also a drawing of its completed appearance.

4. Shields and skull worked in stone; part of the decoration of the roof of the temple of Huitzilopochtli. Also serpent heads from the pyramid body and other local objects.

5. Tunnels allow one to see the various superimpositions.

Xochimilco (So-chee-meel-ko)

About 15 miles southeast of the downtown area, Xochimilco is one of the most popular tourist attractions. Anciently it was an Indian settlement and, later, a refuge from the Toltecs following the fall of Tula. One of the Chichimec tribes, the first of seven to invade Anahuac, and cousins to the Aztecs, settled here in the 13th century.

The Xochimilcas increased their arable land by using an ancient process of piling mud upon mat rafts. (As the crops grew on these floating gardens, the roots eventually took hold, and created small islands.) They developed a thriving trade in green goods with the island capital of the Aztecs. When the lake was drained, the constantly enlarged raft-islands and the canals dividing them remained to become a colorful recreation area. Nothing floats there now but canoes and gondolas.

At war with the Aztecs for 100 years, these people joined with Cortez against them, but later witnessed the burning of their own village and the destruction of their large temple. Vestiges of their ancient highway can be seen on the way to the cemetery where other remains are in poor condition: foundations of priest quarters, a pyramidal step, an observatory and some petroglyphs.

You can visit Xochimilco at any hour of the day, but Mexican family groups go on Sunday afternoon, and that's when the holiday spirit reaches its peak. Along the banks are a number of restaurants where your boatman can dock.

Cerro de la Estrella (Hill of the Star)

In Aztec times, sacred fire rites were carried out every 52 years when all fires were put out in the valley, and priests from each temple came together for the end of the world or the beginning of a new cycle. From the Cerro de la Estrella a new fire was started in the chest cavity of a victim just as the sun was about to rise, and then carried to all parts of the city to re-light the fires and kindle renewed rejoicing for assurance of another 52 years. The hill and cave are south of the town of Ixtapalapa, guarded now by the main altar of a church.

Santa Cecilia Azcatitlán

About two miles from Tenayuca is a small, but nicely detailed pyramid and temple built after the pattern of the great temple at Tenochtitlán. Once a double-staired pyramid topped by two temples, the outer structure and one temple were dismantled by villagers seeking building material for their town. The restored remains reveal the only existing Aztec shrine intact. Like the pyramid of Tenayuca, this one also was built in 52-year stages, and was probably dedicated to the "dying" sun. Two large stone urns at the top of the platform could have held incense or continuously burning flames to the sun god, whose temple remains. Rounded stones, symbolic of skulls, adorn the outer roof of the temple.

A more ancient pyramid still visible beside the main structure was undoubtedly built by the Chichimec, which allowed conquered tribes to worship their old gods.

Near the pyramid a small museum contains Aztec sculpture to the maize, wind, and water gods. Also displayed are a carved stone skull rack from the facade of the main temple, and statues of Chalchiutlicue, the water goddess.

Xochicalco (So-chee-kall-ko)

Xochicalco was one of the first sites to which Mexican archaeologists of the eighteenth century devoted their attention. Alexander von Humboldt, who never visited Xochicalco, availed himself of these pioneer works in order to write a far from accurate description of the site. We now know not only a great deal more about the building described by Humboldt and other scholars of this day, but of various additional ones that have since been explored and in which a great number of objects were found. The ruins of Xochicalco are located 28 miles from Cuernavaca and are situated in the hilltops. The terrain is quite rugged.

The pyramid that was initially uncovered, the Pyramid of the Plumed Serpent, is still outstanding among the monuments at Xochicalco. It is not for its size that it is remarkable—since it is relatively small—but for the low reliefs that originally covered the entire structure. The reliefs on the lower section, comprising a tall sloping base and a wide cornice corresponding to the panel in Teotihuacán-style architecture, show an abundance of motifs. The detail to be seen in this plate represents a plumed serpent—the god Quetzalcoatl—with a skillfully carved head from which a forked tongue protrudes, an undulating body, and a tail terminating in feathers. As with all great ceremonial serpents of Mesoamerica, the

Pyramid of the Plumed Serpent, Xochicalco.

serpent is depicted with an eyebrow as well as a beard under the lower jaw.

One of the spaces formed by the reptile's curves contains hieroglyphs with the sign for fire. The other is even more important because it shows a seated figure holding one hand over the breast and wearing an enormous headdress of plumes. The posture, the design, and the general aspect of this individual recall—even if it is only remotely—a Mayan priest.

On the uppermost level of the ancient city of Xochicalco, built on a moderately high hill, are the remains of a fortress. This would indicate that the site could be defended, unlike Teotihuacán, which is situated in a broad plain. The city of Xochicalco is thought to have been built about the eighth and ninth centuries A.D., and it is estimated to have had between 10 and 20,000 inhabitants. Very little, however, is known about who the inhabitants were. The city lies in the migration route of people moving from the lowlands to the highlands and could have been of Nahuatl or even Mixtec origin. Even Zapotec or Maya glyphs have been found.

On a flat area—and on a lower level than the monument of Quetzalcoatl—is situated the enormous ball court. Sixty-nine meters long, it is much larger than the ball court at Monte Albán but almost identical to the one at Tula, not only in size but in general design. Both are laid out in the customary fashion. The field is in the shape of a capital "I" and flanked on each side by a sloping enbankment

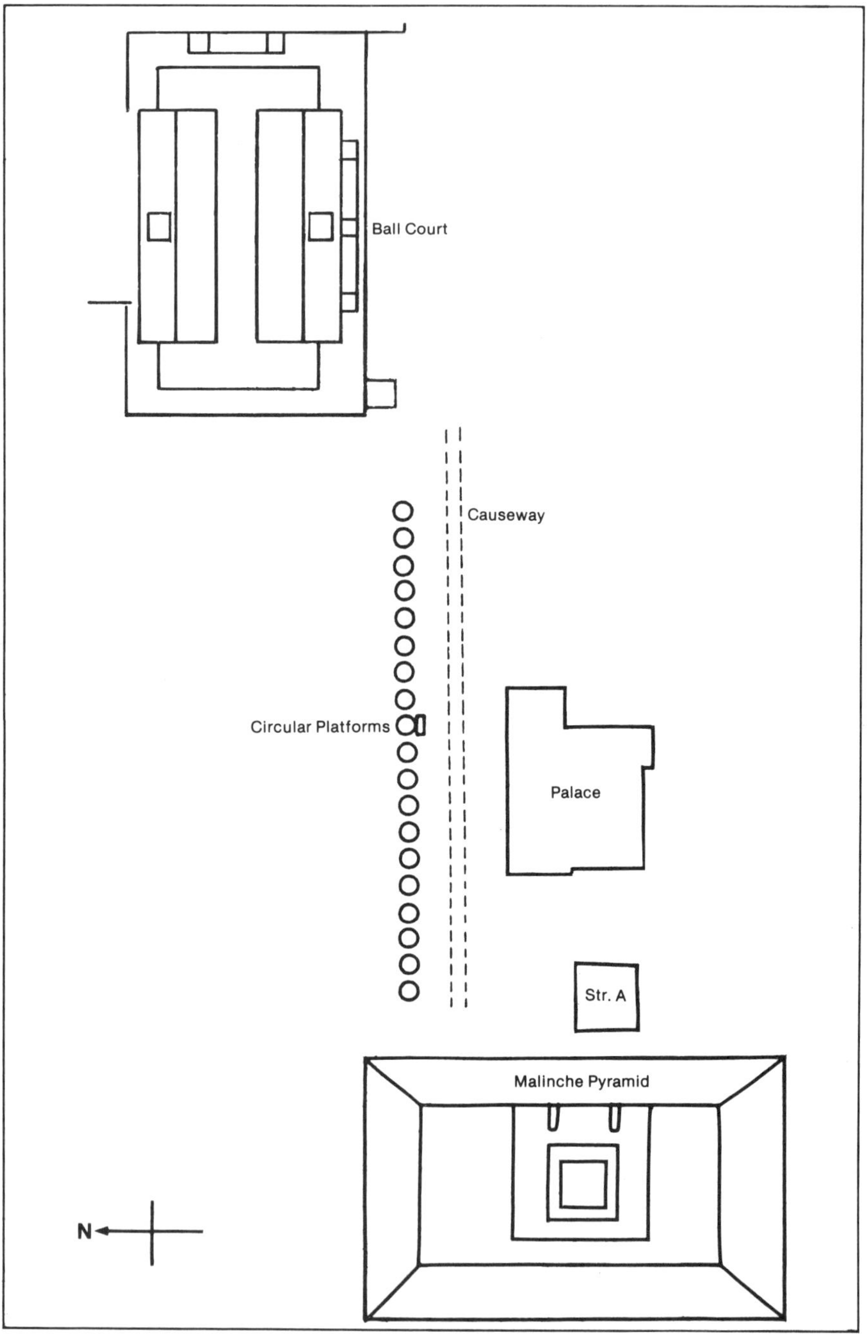

Southwest section of ceremonial center, Xochicalco.

ending in a wall. In the center of the two walls is a large stone ring. It is assumed that the ball was meant to pass through these things, an event that must have been rare indeed if we take into consideration the manner of playing, the size of the ball, and the relatively small orifice. The platforms behind the walls, where the remains of small buildings can still be seen, are not identical: on the north side the natural rock has been utilized; to the south the platform begins on a lower level and follows the slant of the hill. Slopes, porticos, and staircases compensate for this difference.

In the distance can be seen remains of a building known as La Malinche, joined to the ball court by a broad avenue 50 meters long.

Tula

If you are driving into or out of Mexico City via Highway 57 D you might want to see Tula then, rather than making it a special trip. There are several exits off the main road to the town and the archaeological zone. The first one going north out of the city is eight miles past the toll gate, at Kilometer 56. Tula is off to the right on Highway 126, east of Highway 57. You will pass a large petroleum refinery and then come to a small bridge; from this point, the ruins are a short distance to the right beyond the railroad tracks, while the town is straight ahead.

Historians agree that this zone was founded by the Toltecas who had their origins in the destruction of Teotihuacán. The area was settled about A.D. 900. Heirs to the Teotihuacán culture (probably enriched by Maya elements), the Toltecas are described in every historical source as being a wealthy and numerous people, highly skilled in arts and crafts to such a degree that the designation "tolteca" came to mean "wise, skilled, dextrous," rather than simply reference to a nationality.

It was here in Tula that the usurper of the Fair God Quetzalcoatl came into being. The nomadic Toltec chieftain Mixcoatl, or "Cloud Smoke" was killed in battle, but he had a son, Ce Acatl Topiltzin, born after his death. This son, who was reared by his grandparents, eventually established himself at Tula.

> Tradition holds that this enterprising monarch, after imposing on his Nahuatl-speaking Chichimec subjects the cult of Quetzalcoatl, or the feathered serpent, also assumed the name of the deity. This tradition is supported by a rock carving at Tula depicting Quetzalcoatl and bearing a date corresponding to A.D. 968.[6]

Ce Acatl Topiltzin not only assumed the name but also the attributes of the god supposedly becoming deified. In the middle of the tenth century, Topiltzin / Quetzalcoatl left Tula and, with a retinue of followers, traveled to the Gulf Coast but he promised to return. It is now believed that he continued on to the Yucatán where he took over the area of Chichén Itzá.

After he left the center declined and fell easy prey to Aztec warriors who swept in to burn and raze the city in A.D. 1156.

Structures in Tula seemed to have been built more for show than durability. They were constructed of large rocks without mortar and with weak adobe walls. Most of the pre-Columbian Mesoamerican sculpture is religious in character with art work representing gods. At Tula, however, four-fifths of the sculpture represent human beings linked with military might.

Standing as lone sentinels in this destroyed city are the four 15-foot, eight-and-one-half-ton colossi, or atlantes. At one time there was also a huge temple that crowned a pyramid. That entrance was flanked by two massive columns in the shape of plumed serpents. Today all that remains are the pyramid platform with four huge, ornately carved columns and the four gigantic statues representing warriors or crusaders of Quetzalcoatl in the guise of Venus, the evening star. These atlantes and columns once supported the roof

The atlantes and pillars of Tula.

of the temple. Each warrior wears a headdress formed of a wide, star-studded band terminating in a feather cluster. Originally the faces were painted and obsidian inlays filled the eye sockets and partly opened mouths. The figures are garbed in short, embroidered tunics topped by elaborate breastplates in the form of a butterfly. On each breast is a clasp on which appears a human face emerging from a disc surrounded by four entwined serpents. The warriors' bracelets and sandals are also adorned with plumed serpents.

In their left hands they carry an atlatl or dart thrower and in the other a sheaf of arrows. The two atlantes in the middle are originals, while the one on the left is a copy.

The pillars bear the likeness of a personage who had been identified as Quetzalcoatl, along with a bundle of arrows.

This ruin was inhabited several centuries past the close of Book of Mormon history, but it is important because it shows the continuation of the legend of Quetzalcoatl even though the legend becomes more distorted as time goes on.

Pyramids of Teotihuacán

There are many tours for tourists to this famous site northeast of Mexico City. It is an easy drive, but if you are tired of driving a tour may be more relaxing.

Starting at the intersection of Paseo de Reforma and Avenida Insurgentes, go northward. You will pass a large building distinguished by a stunning mural dealing with Revolution and Reform, the Institutional Revolutionary Party (Partido Revolucionario Instucional or PRI). The Mexican National Railways (Ferrocarriles Nacionales de Mexico) is not far beyond, then a few blocks farther is a steep, triangular building which is a housing center. When you come to the La Raza interchange dedicated to the Mexican race, follow the signs marked "Insurgentes." There are signs directing you to the pyramids which are approximately 20 miles from the edge of the city. The toll road is best, so follow the signs marked "Cuota" (toll).

Since this immense 40-acre site in the Valley of Mexico is only about 30 miles north of Mexico City, it is probably the most visited archaeological zone in Mexico. When the Aztecs, who came in several centuries after its abandonment, first saw it they were so impressed they gave it its name, which means "The City of the Gods."

The Teotihuacanos present a great mystery to historians because no one knows their origin or what language they spoke. One archaeologist suggests that they are inheritors of the Olmeca tradition.[7] This may be because of the prevalence of shells from the Gulf

Coast (land of the Olmecs) in the sculptural ornamentation of the Temple of Quetzalcoatl. They also had a common calendrical system with the Nahuas, the Olmecs and the Maya. The signs denoting days, months, and years were indicated by them in varying symbols.

Evidence indicates that a culture was present about 1500 B.C., and the Teotihuacanos began to settle there by 100 B.C. During the period from the year One to A.D. 150, the city grew rapidly and had approximately 30,000 inhabitants. Guidebook author Valades writes: "Building is the foremost activity, more than twenty separate ceremonial compounds are built during this phase, besides the pyramids of the Sun and the Moon."[8] It was a religious center and drew pilgrims from as far away as Yucatán and Central America. During the same period it was also the most active trading center in the Mexican highlands.

The layout of the city is unique for pre-Columbian sites. The main axis of the city is the 130-foot-wide Avenue of the Dead. It was called this because it was believed that the mounds flanking it contained tombs. The avenue was designed to connect two principal groups of buildings—about one and one-half miles apart—with the Temple of the Moon at one end and the Temple of Quetzalcoatl at the other. On the east is the majestic Pyramid of the Sun.

Avenue of the Dead, Teotihuacán.

Pyramid of the Sun, Teotihuacán.

Pyramid of the Moon, Teotihuacán.

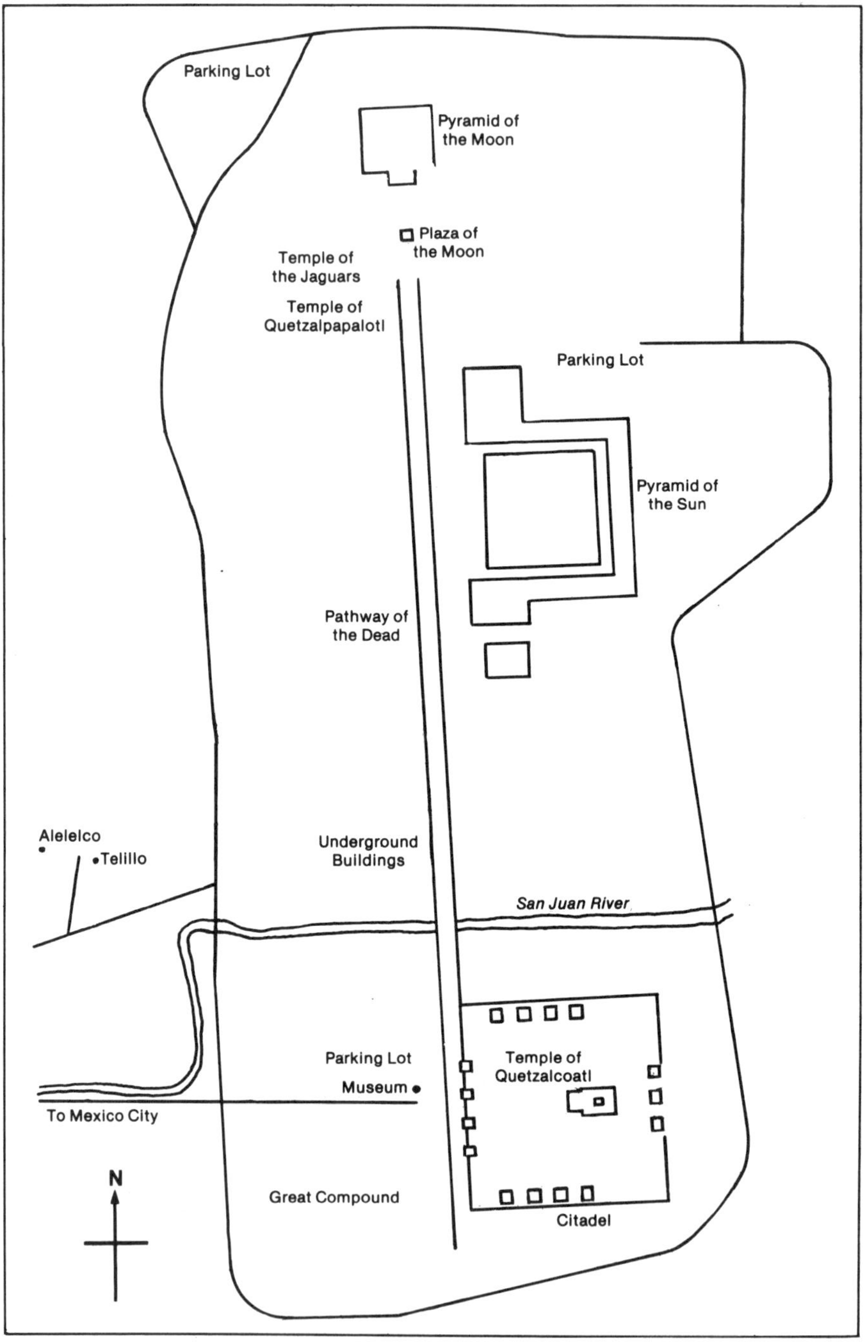

Teotihuacán

Temple of Quetzalcoatl, Teotihuacán.

The Plumed Serpent, Quetzalcoatl, Teotihuacán.

Quite possibly the principal buildings of the city are arranged according to a highly complicated astronomical scheme. Each temple was so placed that the sun's rays would strike a portion of it on a given day and at a given season. Such an arrangement is part of the calendrical system that played so dominant a role in ancient Mexican life.

The Pyramid of the Sun is about 720 by 760 feet at its base, and it rises in five great elevations to a height of about 216 feet. One researcher suggests that it was constructed as a base for a temple which probably crowned the pyramid during the first two centuries after Christ, and that it may have been used as a center for true worship of Jesus Christ. The "sun" worship came as doctrine for later apostate groups.[9]

The Pyramid of the Moon is smaller than the Pyramid of the Sun, but they are on the same level because the Moon is built on a higher level.

The Temple of Quetzalcoatl was constructed around A.D. 200. The worship of the Fair God, represented by the plumed or feathered serpent, is undeniable in Teotihuacán. The large structure here has many of the plumed serpents projecting out of a wall. Apostasy had started to set in by this time, however, as there are—along with the serpent—sculptures of the rain god, Tlaloc. This god is represented as a masked countenance with goggle eyes, protruding fangs, and drooping moustache.

The period from A.D. 200 to 450 is the period of greatest splendor. Many temples, including the Temple of the Plumed Shells and the Palace of Quetzalpapalotl, were constructed during this time. The latter is a courtyard with pillars carved in calendrical motifs and the quetzal-butterfly surrounded by symbols related to water. A tunnel leads under this Patio of the Columns to the Palace of the Jaguars where colorful murals of two enormous felines with feathered heads are blowing on a seashell held on the forepaws. Because it is protected from the elements, this mural still has its color (or it is possible it has been retouched). All of Teotihuacán was once this colorful.

"The large number of temples dating to the period of the great apostasy after A.D. 200, plus the development of a highly classed society, all fit into the Book of Mormon description. This may indeed have been a center for the apostate sects which gave out sacred information to the unworthy and which adorned their temples with all manner of precious things."[10]

During this era inhabitants numbered between 100,000 and 200,000. There are great evidences of trade and influence with all of

Mesoamerica, especially at Kaminaljuyú (now Guatemala City), the surrounding area of the highlands of Guatemala, as well as the Pacific coastal regions of the states of Chiapas and Oaxaca.

About A.D. 650 to 750 Teotihuacán was abandoned. No one knows why. The burning of the buildings in the center of the city sometime in the seventh century seems to indicate a violent end. However, there is no definite evidence that this was so. The people who emerged from the city were called the Toltecas, and some say that after they left Teotihuacán they moved to Tula some 83 miles north of Mexico City. When the Spaniards found Teotihuacán they felt it was a threat so they destroyed it, stone by stone, and used the resulting rubble to fill in canals and to form foundations for new structures.

Cholula

Near the city of Puebla is a large man-made mountain where we find the Pyramid of Cholula, considered to be the largest in the world. The early Spanish destroyed most of the ancient structure and used the materials to build the town of Puebla. After serious excavation was begun, archaeologists found near the base of this tremendous structure many evidences of the building style used by the master builders who constructed it. It is thought by some scholars that there were as many as six superpositions of buildings and that the innermost structure was erected as early as 2000 B.C.

The pyramid is 187 feet high, with its base covering approximately 44 acres. Although not as tall as the Pyramid of Cheops, King of Egypt, it is almost twice as long as Cheops, and therefore probably had a larger mass. It took many thousands of workmen to build this magnificent structure, which the people called "Tlachihualtepetl," meaning "man-made mountain."

The city of Cholula at the time of the Spanish conquest was much larger than it is today. At that time it is reported to have had approximately 40,000 houses and up to 200 temples set atop the surrounding hills. These "pagan" temples, however, were destroyed by the conquering Spanish and then built over with the Catholic churches, with 365 of these churches being built using ruins from the temples as building materials. Today the population of Cholula is a mere 15 to 20,000 with most of these churches slowly disintegrating.

The largest Catholic Church was constructed over the exact spot atop the giant pyramid where there was a building for worship purposes.

Excavation of the pyramid began in 1931 and, in order to establish its chronology, over four miles of tunnels were made through

The Pyramid of Cholula.

the pyramid at which time an intricate system of passages was discovered. Today these tunnels are electrified so that travelers can enter and study the different stages of development. In one of these tunnels a burial section, apart from the main structure, was discovered.

There are remains of many murals at Cholula. The most spectacular of these is located in an interior structure on the west side of the Great Plaza which was built sometime between the second and third centuries. It depicts a ceremonial drinking scene, and subjects of the painting include men, women, dogs, and even insects. The mural itself is over 150 feet long.

Little is known of the people who inhabited Cholula, their language, or even the extent of their political control, but we do know that the great culture affected other cultures as far away as Tulum, in Quintana Roo, and Santa Rita in Belize. It was once a powerful city and was an arts and crafts center specializing in pottery. Civilization was thriving there during Book of Mormon times.

Mexico City to Veracruz (Highway 150 D, 275 miles)

The majority of this highway is a divided toll road through the mountains. Seventy-five miles east of Mexico City is the turnoff for Cholula. Continue on to the lovely coast town of Veracruz. If you have time, go to the central plaza at night and watch the Mexicans enjoy themselves in this beautiful square. The restaurants have tables on the covered sidewalks, so everyone sits and eats or drinks and visits while bands play and children play under the watchful eyes of their parents. Weekends are the best time to be there.

An Alternate Route to Veracruz

Instead of going to Veracruz via Mexico City, or for a change of scenery on the return trip home, take the coast Highway 180 north of Veracruz which passes by the ruins of Zempoala and El Tajín on the way to Tampico and the Texas border.

Zempoala is a little way north of Veracruz and was the first town where Hernán Cortez became friendly with the Indians.

If going to El Tajín, continue on Highway 180 to Poza Rica and watch for the signs that lead to a road off the highway to the ruins.

If you are going on to Tampico, be prepared for a long wait for the ferry. This is a very colorful drive in the winter. The lush green trees are a lovely background for the bright orange tangerines in winter months. The road between McAllen and Veracruz is not as good as Highway 57, but it is much more interesting.

Zempoala

Located on the Gulf Coast Highway 180, just north of Veracruz, Zempoala was a Totonac town which now occupies an archaeological zone of three square miles between the Actopan and the San Carlos Chachalacas rivers. With changes taking place in the course of the San Carlos Chachalacas, sections of the ancient city have been isolated and modern streets have invaded the ceremonial city. The Totonacs moved in to occupy Zempoala (also known as Sempoala and Cempoala) about the end of the Classic period, around A.D. 800.

Historically, Zempoala is important because it was the first town Hernán Cortez and his soldiers entered after they landed at nearby Villa Rica. Bernál Diaz was in the entourage, and he described their reaction to the town: "We continued our march, and as we got among the houses and saw what a large town it was, larger than any we had seen, and struck with admiration. It looked like a garden with luxuriant vegetation, and the streets were so full of men and women who had come to see us that we gave thanks to God at having discovered such a country." [11]

When their scouts, who were on horseback, reached a great plaza with courts, they thought the buildings were covered with silver. The structures had recently been whitewashed and were brilliant in the sunshine.

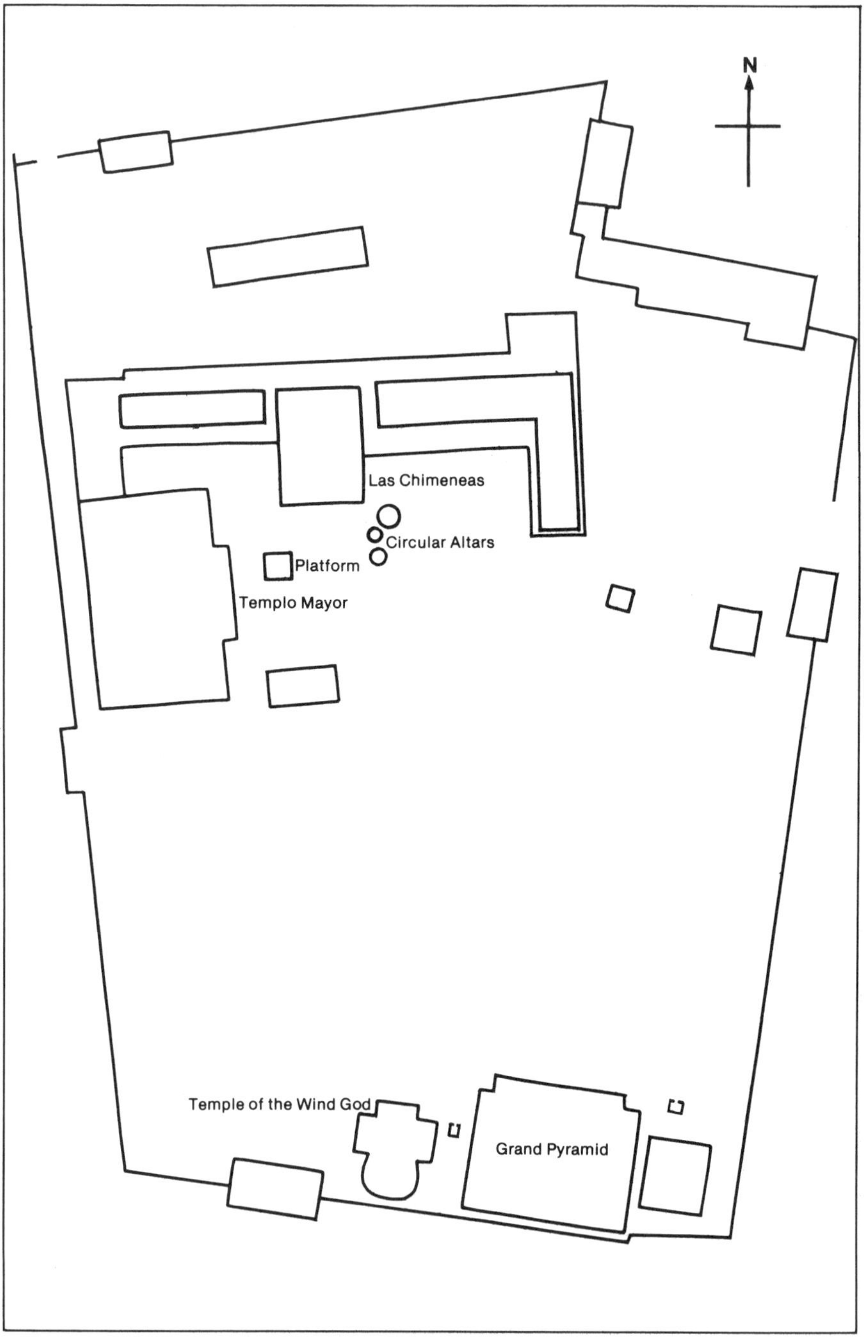

Section of Zempoala

The mayor of the town told Cortez that they had recently been brought under the yoke of Moctezuma and his governors, and that all their gold and jewels had been carried off and he and his people were so grieviously oppressed that they dared do nothing without Moctezuma's orders, for he was the Lord over many cities and countries and ruled countless vassals and armies of warriors.[12]

The atmosphere of oppression enabled Cortez to persuade these Indians to join him in his march to Mexico and domination of the Aztecs.

Today, the zone has an appearance of a large plaza surrounded by crenellated walls. Inside are several structures: a 36-foot High Temple; the Temple of the Chimneys; a building known as the Great Pyramid; the Temple of the Little Faces; and the Temple of the Wind God, also known as the God of the Air, which is one of the few extant circular temples associated with the cult of Quetzalcoatl as god of the wind.

El Tajín

El Tajín is on the gulf coast of Mexico, about halfway between the cities of Veracruz and Tampico, ten miles south of Poza Rica on Highway 180. It is 30 kilometers from the Gulf of Mexico and is only slightly above sea level in a hot and humid climate. A compact group of temples, buildings, and palaces indicates influence from the Teotihuacán, Mayan, and Oaxaca cultures. However, some innovations make this ruin singularly attractive. The ornamental sculptured design of interlocking scrolls, along with other decorative designs, represents some of the finest sculpture in pre-Columbian America.

While the majority of the buildings still await excavation, the principal building, the Temple of the Niches, is one of the best known in Mexico. The temple, about 36 meters wide on each side and 25 meters high, is constructed in a ziggurat fashion. Each story has an extended panel and a projecting cornice with panels decorated with niches or indentations. The latest research concludes that these niches, which were painted red with blue frames, were always empty and for decorative purposes only. There are even niches underneath the stairway at the front of the pyramid, indicating that the stairway was superimposed on the building. It is interesting to note that the number of niches totals 365 which seems to correlate in some way with the number of days in the year.

A tall pole was used in a ceremonial game called "voladores" (flying dancers). Five men participated; one stayed at the top of the pole while the others attached themselves to ropes, unwinding themselves from the top and assuming a bird-like flight in their descent.

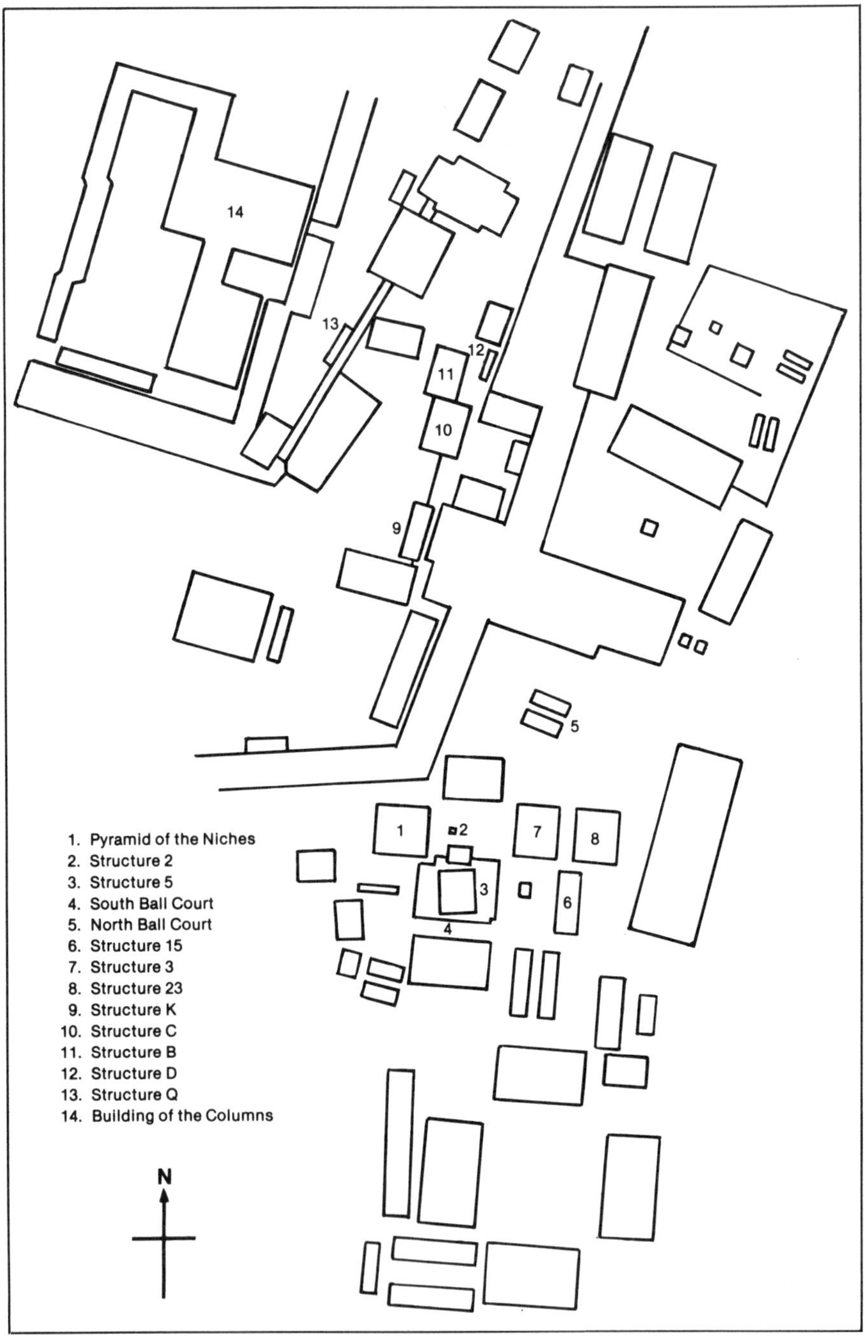
14
13
12
11
10
9
5
1
2
3
4
6
7
8
1. Pyramid of the Niches
2. Structure 2
3. Structure 5
4. South Ball Court
5. North Ball Court
6. Structure 15
7. Structure 3
8. Structure 23
9. Structure K
10. Structure C
11. Structure B
12. Structure D
13. Structure Q
14. Building of the Columns
N

El Tajín

The Pyramid of the Niches, El Tajín

The Pyramid of the Niches, El Tajín

There are several ball courts at Tajín, with sculptured figures on the walls depicting various ceremonies attached to the playing of this ancient religious game. Friezes and panels on the walls depict ritual scenes.

Found on the site are other buildings, called Lesser Tajíns, decorated with friezes, panels, and facades. Stone carvings are also numerous. Another interesting and most unusual building is the Building of the Columns which is adorned with Greek crosses.

Veracruz to Villahermosa (Highway 180, 295 miles)

This is the old Olmec (Jaredite) country where oil has been discovered. In some areas the traffic from the oil refineries make the trip less than enjoyable; however, there are some compensations.

Go into the little town of Santiago Tuxtla, a lovely little village in the Tuxtla Mountains. The town is nestled at the foot of a beautiful hill, Cerro Vigia (Vi-hia). Brigham Young University researchers have done an extensive study, comparing the hill and its surroundings with the Book of Mormon, and they believe this could be the Hill Cumorah and also the Jaredite Hill Ramah. In the town an interesting museum with a huge stone head from La Venta in the patio is well worth a visit.

From Santiago Tuxtla, continue on Highway 180, pass the Isthmus of Tehuantepec which is believed by some to be the "narrow neck of land" mentioned in the Book of Mormon, separating the Land Southward from the Land Northward. Along this area the maps show the La Venta ruins, but the oil companies have taken over this coastline. The artifacts have been taken to the La Venta Outdoor Museum in Villahermosa.

La Venta Museum

To see this unique and important museum in Villahermosa, continue on Highway 180, which is Boulevard Grijalva, into town. Pass Avenida 27 de Febrero (in Mexico streets are named after important historical dates), Paseo Usumacinto, and turn right at Paseo Tabasco. The entrance to the park is across the street from the Hotel Cencali on Tabasco, a short distance from the intersection.

There are 33 monuments of the Olmeca culture. These include stelae, monoliths (some weighing 30 tons), and one of the famous huge stone heads, all placed in lovely park surroundings similar to that where they were found. These ruins are important because of their age, and some have carvings of bearded men with Hebraic noses.

A great stone head of La Venta.

When leaving Villahermosa ("beautiful town"), you cross the Grijalva River which could be the River Sidon in the Book of Mormon according to some BYU researchers.

Villahermosa to Escarcega (Highway 186, 183 miles)

Out of Villahermosa, follow the signs to the Palenque Ruins. The junction is a little over seventy miles from the city. Before going in to Palenque, you need to look ahead a bit and decide whether to go to that ruin now or wait until the return trip from the Yucatán Peninsula. You will be traveling this same road on the return trip.

From Chetumal on the Caribbean coast back to Villahermosa, there are no accommodations except gas stations on this 300-mile stretch of road. The highway is straight and fairly good, but it is a long time between hotels or trailer parks. These facilities are available at Palenque which is 22 miles off the highway, so you might want to visit this beautiful and important ruin on the way back.

Palenque (Pah-LEN-kay)

This fabulous ruin was so hidden in the jungle that no modern man knew of its existence until 1773. Even then, it was discovered and "lost" several times until 1841 when John L. Stephens and Frederick Catherwood arrived and described it in detail. The region around Palenque has the highest average rainfall in all of Mexico, so

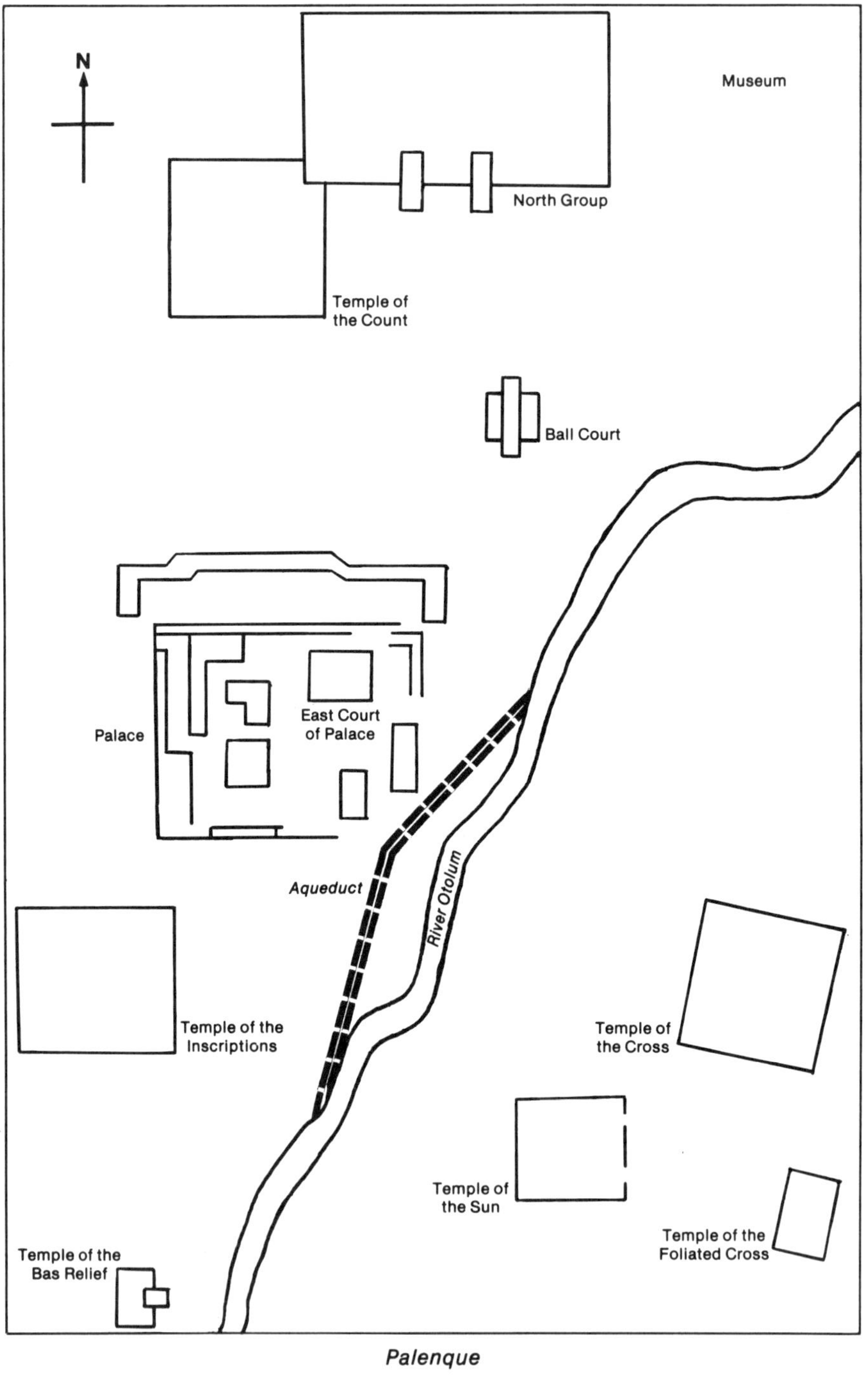
N
Museum
North Group
Temple of
the Count
Ball Court
Palace
East Court
of Palace
Aqueduct
River Otolum
Temple of the
Inscriptions
Temple of
the Cross
Temple of
the Sun
Temple of the
Foliated Cross
Temple of the
Bas Relief

Palenque

even today men work with their machetes to keep the area free from the enveloping jungle growth.

Located on a side road 22 miles off Highway 186 and 75 miles east of Villahermosa, this is the most beautiful of the ancient ruins in Mexico. Only 34 structures have been opened of the estimated 500 that are scattered over the area.

Palenque dates from 300 B.C. Pottery sherds are all that are left in the area since the jungle moisture destroys everything but stone, and even that deteriorates in time. This Mayan site reached its zenith around A.D. 700, and between the years A.D. 1000 and 1500 it was so completely abandoned and lost to the jungle that it was lost to the memory of man as well. When it was flourishing, Palenque must have been quite a spectacular sight, with the multi-colored painted structures against the green jungle background.

The name Palenque is Spanish and means "palisade" or "place of war." The true Mayan name is unknown. A modern road takes you to the very center of this complex of ornate buildings where one can still see evidence of recent diggings. Hills surrounding the ancient buildings reveal their man-made characteristics, and one suspects that the entire story has not yet been told.

The Palace is the largest and most impressive structure at Palenque. The tower, with its pagoda look, was destroyed before the first European saw it and was reconstructed scientifically in 1955. The palace complex is set upon an artificial platform 30 feet high and 300 feet long by 240 feet deep, thus affording a commanding view all the way to the ocean over the flat plains in front. Good examples of the Mayan corbelled arch (it has no keystone) are visible in the outer corridor around the complex. The inner maze consists of four large odd-size open-air patios. One of these is a sunken plaza where, flanking the staircase of "Casa A," are nine figures sculpted on large slabs.

Six main temples have been discovered to date. The most important of these is the Temple of Inscriptions. Inside this temple, below ground level, is a burial tomb that contained the body of an ancient and honored leader placed there some 1300 years ago. (See inset, p. 72.) This find illustrates the fact that the pyramids of the Americas did occasionally serve as tombs as is the case of the pyramids in the Old World. On the surface of this tomb is engraven the Tree of Life insignia in the shape of a cross. A replica of the tomb is in the National Museum of Anthropology in Mexico City.

Sculptured figures and hieroglyphs cover many surfaces of the inner and outer walls of these buildings and courtyards. Scholars have

The Palace of Palenque

dated these buildings back to before the time of Christ, and some researchers also believe this could be the cradle of the Mayan civilization.

Three tablets that were originally located in the Temple of the Cross were broken and moved several times but they have now been gathered together and are on display in the Mexican National Museum of Anthropology in Mexico City. The complete panel contains long rows of hieroglyphs on both sides and two standing figures facing the central carving of a tree in the form of a cross, thus giving the temple its name.

As one gazes over the countryside from atop the Temple of the Cross or the Temple of the Sun, one can see the vast plains of Tabasco and, on clear days, the Gulf of Mexico.

The Ostolum River flows through the center of the ruins of Palenque and was a source of water supply for the community. An artificial bed in the river suggests that it might have been used for bathing, swimming, or even religious rites. At certain places the stream disappears underground and flows through man-made culverts. The roofs of these culverts are supported by the Mayan "false arch." Although not as versatile as the true arch, it serves as a very convenient way of covering long chambers. An example of the use of this arch is found in the Temple of the Sun.

A reflection of a magnificent culture, Palenque stands as a mysterious and exquisite monument to the ancient and very civilized inhabitants of America.

Another reason for considering when to see the ruins of Palenque is the decision of which road to take to Oaxaca. You have a choice of three roads. The one south out of Palenque goes through beautiful countryside with picturesque waterfalls, Agua Azul and De Mizol Ha, goes up and through wonderfully steep mountains to Ocosingo, then on to charming San Cristobal las Casas, home of the Chamula Indians. Some of this road may be under construction, but most of the highway is new and very good. Highway 195 leads off 186 near (but bypassing) Villahermosa to Chiapa de Corzo, and Highway 185 crosses the Tehuantepec Peninsula to Highway 190 / 200.

It is important for you to obtain the most recent and detailed map since the road system is being improved all the time.

Izapa

If you wish to go to Guatemala, you can take Highway 190 and enter at Cuidad Cuauhtemoc. However, if you take the coastal road of Highway 200, you can see the important ruins of Izapa between Tapachula and the Guatemalan border.

There are two parts to this ruin. One is on the left side of the road going south, but the part where Stela 5 is located is on the right side of the road. There is a little dirt road that turns off the main road across from the visable archaeological zone on the left. There are caretakers of this zone, so you will have to ask directions to the Stela 5 complex which is about a mile from the highway and rather hard to find. There are several stelae in the field, but they are not identified. Stela 5 has a canopy over it, and can be recognized by the drawings or carvings of the Tree of Life.

Occupied during Book of Mormon time period, Izapa lies between the city of Tapachula, Mexico, and the Guatemalan border, off Highway 200, amid the green hills of the Pacific lowland of the state of Chiapas.

Dated between 400 B.C. and A.D. 300, this is an important archaeological zone because it bridges the Olmec and Maya cultures. The sculptures found here show a distinct style which has not been found at other sites as far away as Tres Zapotes on the Gulf Coast of Veracruz and at Kaminaljuyú in the Guatemalan highlands. This style of art is considered a link between the Pre-Classic and Classic periods and is believed to have been derived from the earlier Olmec style.

Izapan art is the first to include two crucial elements of the Classic Maya (A.D. 300 to A.D. 900)—the calendar and hieroglyphic writing. In 1962, The New World Archaeological Foundation from Brigham Young University began a program of excavation and restoration which lasted four years. They discovered a thin fragment of polished limestone from an Izapan site. Engraved on it are bars and dots—number symbols—in the sequence that ancient Mesoamericans employed to record dates in their complex calendar. Though incomplete, this date can be equated to December 5, 36 B.C. If the reading is correct, the little slab bears the earliest recorded date in the New World. The Classic Maya, using the very same system, would not carve their earliest known date until A.D. 292.

Replica of the Tree of Life Stone.
Stela 5, Izapa.

At Izapa, there are 80 platforms of clay faced with river cobbles along with nearly 250 upright stone monuments, some with round altars in front. On one of these stelae, bearing a date of A.D. 126, is carved the Tree of Life. Dr. Ross T. Christensen, former Chairman of the Department of Anthropology, BYU, has made an intensive study of this engraving and finds that it has similarities with the story in the Book of Mormon and with the Mesopotamia Tree of Life representations. Regarding this "Stele 5," he says it is ". . . the most direct and striking evidence in support of the Book of Mormon which has yet come forth from the science of archaeology. I do not know who carved this sculpture—whether the artist was a Nephite, a

Lamanite, or of some other lineage—but whoever did it was beyond any doubt familiar with the story of Lehi's vision of the Tree of Life as recounted in 1 Nephi, Chapter 8." [13]

Dr. M. Wells Jakeman of BYU has made a lifetime study of Stela 5. A replica of the stele is in the Museum of Peoples and Cultures, Seventh North and First East, Provo, Utah.

The road (186) from Palenque junction to the junction at Escarcega is straight with nothing special to see.

Escarcega to Merida (junction of Highways 261 and 186, 250 miles)

This is the beginning of the Yucatán Peninsula with Highway 261 going north along the Gulf of Mexico to Campeche, a large, modern town with all accommodations. Continue east on 261 to Hopelchén and go north toward Mérida. This area has many important ruins, so plan your day accordingly.

After the road turns north at Hopelchén, continue on until you see the signs to the road on the right where the Puuc ruins Sayil (or Zayil), X-la-pak (Shlah-PAHK), and Labna are located. The area is named after a range of hills in this area of Yucatán. After viewing these ruins, return on the same road to Highway 261.

A little way north from the Sayil road junction on 261 are the ruins of Kabah, right alongside the road.

The major ruins of Uxmal (OOS-mal) are about 18 kilometers north of Kabah.

To see all the ruins in this area will take most of a day. The gates are open from 8 a.m. to 5 p.m., so it is necessary to plan ahead. It is only 50 miles from Uxmal to Mérida.

Sayil

The construction and habitation of Sayil began sometime around A.D. 800. Many mounds are apparent but three buildings remain to testify of the people—the Mirador, the ball court, and the palace. In a bad state of preservation, the Sayil palace still reveals the great skill of the workmen.

The palace, which is the dominant monument, is a distinctive Puuc design (intricate ornamentation on the upper half of the facade, and plain on the lower half). It has three stories in stepped formation, the upper ones being supported by a solid fill set back from the floor below. They are connected in front by a great stairway of three flights, allowing access to terraces on each level. The lower facade—rather plain—has adornments of stucco or rows of little columns above the level of the doors. The middle story, by far the most elaborate, has a series of little columns on the mouldings, between the

The Great Palace of Sayil

doors, and on the frieze. At the corners the characteristic masks may be seen, while in the middle of each section a carved panel shows a god descending—a frequent figure in Mesoamerica—flanked by two serpents in outline. The third story above each of the seven doors (five at the front and one on each side) has the figure of a human in stucco placed on a pedestal.

The whole structure is characterized by the apparent desire of the builders for rich ornamentation contrasted with extensive plain surfaces. Not without justification do various scholars consider the Palace of Sayil to be one of the great triumphs of Mayan art and architecture. This is especially true when it is realized that the palace was built over a long period of time, and in stages, yet it still became one unit and all parts work together to form a harmonious whole.

The lowest story of the palace is divided into three wings. Each of these was built at a different time. This is obvious from the great amount of difference in their decorative details. The second story was, however, built at one time and, as previously mentioned, its facade is by far the most elaborate. The third level was also built at one time and in such a way that it fit together perfectly with the rest of the palace making it a well-organized and quite impressive structure.

We do not know who built or inhabited this vast seventy-room structure. The city, like Labna and Kabah, seems to have been abandoned before the arrival of Toltec influence in the tenth century A.D. There were not dated inscriptions here (or at least none that have been found), but in neighboring Puuc cities all the latest dates are around the middle of the ninth century except that of Uxmal, which gives the year 909.

Xlapak (Shlah-PAHK)

This is the smallest of the three ceremonial sites found on the side road off Highway 261, south of Uxmal. Sayil, Labna, and Xlapak are of the same time period (around A.D. 900).

Xlapak is one of the ancient Puuc cities only partially excavated, but a beautiful corner of the palace, with its three superimposed masks of the god of rain, can be seen. Short columns separate the decorated area above from the plain area below. In the center the masks assume a geometric form, while to their left can be seen the beginning of a "xicolcoliuhqui," the fret that in a multitude of variations represents a stylized serpent and was used in all Mesoamerica from the end of the Pre-Classic period.

The photograph on the following page evokes the romantic atmosphere of drawings from the middle of the nineteenth century in which wild plants are shown growing in profusion over stones carved with so much effort and application in ancient times, with the plants slowly destroying the masonry until finally it falls to the ground.

Masks of the rain god Chac at the Temple of Xlapak.

John Lloyd Stephens illustrates his second book, *Incidents of Travel in Yucatán*, which appeared in 1843, with numerous drawings made by that enterprising London architect Frederick Catherwood, who accompanied him on his trips. Current tastes, the solitude of the ruins, and his profound interest in the ancient Maya and their works led Catherwood to populate his accurate drawings with trees and plants, which, far from weakening their archaeological value, renders them more realistic.

Much mystery surrounds these unexcavated ruins, and the beautiful vegetation and foliage covering the buildings make the scene even more intriguing.

Labna

Another Mayan city in the Puuc style is Labna, only a few miles from the neighboring cities of Kabah, Sayil, Xlapak and Uxmal. Labna, like its close neighbors, dates from the late Classic period (Circa

A.D. 500 to A.D. 900).The land configuration at Labna is generally flat with the exception of a low ring of hills surrounding the central ceremonial area. These hills have been artificially terraced and leveled.

Labna can be divided into three main groups—the northernmost group being the palace group which limits the north side of the main plaza. The lower level of the palace group is divided into three courtyards each being flanked by a long palace-type building. The most important building at Labna is the great palace.

A long highway paved with stones leads in a southerly direction from the palace across the main plaza toward the group of which El Mirador forms part. The front part of the temple is divided into three rooms—a central one flanked by two others. Behind the room in the middle is a sanctuary, roofed with the Mayan vault. Although much simpler than the facades of Palenque, this one features standing figures somewhat larger than natural size with big, ornamental motifs in the middle. All the statues were placed on pedestals, but very little remains of these today.

Roof-combed Temple near Labna.

A notable feature is the enormous roof comb more than four meters in height, which gives the temple a lofty and imposing appearance. This roof comb must have been very elaborate when first built.

There remains on it today a number of stones projecting out from the rest of the comb which at one time supported large stucco masks. This is referred to by John Lloyd Stevens, who visited Labna in 1841. He describes the comb as being completely covered with stucco relief sculptures which included a row of death heads at the top, two lines of human figures just below, and a colossal seated figure over the central doorway. Above the central figure was a large ball with a human figure beside it and another below. The figures and ornaments on the wall were painted, as traces of bright color were still visible. Unlike the combs at Palenque, the one here is not placed on the transverse axis of the building; it is aligned with the facade, so that from the front of the building it looks like a prolongation of the latter, and it consists of only a single wall. This type of roof comb, while it corresponds to the Classic period, is characteristic of the Yucatán zone and not the zone of the great rivers, as is the case of those in Palenque.

In Yucatán the ever-more-frequent use of the Mayan vault led to the erection of enormous vaulted doorways such as those of the Governor's Palace at Uxmal. In Kabah this is carried even further, for at this site there is an independent Mayan gateway that puts one in mind of the triumphal arch. The following photograph shows an arch of like monumental proportions at Labna, but it is not quite independent since it serves as a doorway between two ceremonial patios.

The Triumphal Arch of Labna.

This huge ornamental gateway has a small roof comb above the main opening, as if it were a temple. The chambers on either side are in classic Puuc Style: the lower part of the facade is entirely plain, while the upper part is decorated with the characteristic lattice pattern with models of huts in the middle that perhaps formerly contained sculpture.

Kabah

In the midst of several nearby ruins, Kabah is on Highway 261, 65 miles south of Mérida. This is a Mayan city of the late Classic period (c. A.D. 500 to A.D. 900). During the ninth and tenth centuries this section of Yucatán supported the densest population in the northern half of the peninsula, a population which gathered around many ceremonial centers according to explorer Sylvanus Morley.[14] Kabah was the second largest of these centers and was located nine miles southeast of Uxmal and connected to it by a stone causeway. It is embellished with an archway just west of the main complex of buildings.

The builders of Kabah made extensive use of columns with capitals, or motifs, decorated lintels and groups of columns.

A change from the Puuc design, the most interesting structure at Kabah is the Palace of the Masks (Kodes-pope or Codz Pop "rolled mat"). It is 151 feet long and has a facade completely decorated with masks of the ancient rain god Chac which is identified by its long hooked, or curled, nose. Originally there were 270 of these masks, but now they are mostly in a state of ruin. Enough remains to give us an idea of what they were like, however.

In contrast to the Governor's Palace at Uxmal, the Codz Pop has rooms on different levels and possibly was designed to have two stories with one set back behind the other. But the second story was never built; instead, an enormous roof comb was erected upon the nucleus that had been prepared. It is possible that after the facade was finished, the builders were disappointed and decided to complete the structure in a simpler fashion than had originally been planned.

The decoration on the facade of the Codz Pop is, in fact, overpowering. Rows of the enormous masks cover every square foot of surface, and not only the front but also the sides and perhaps the wall behind were covered with showy and overcrowded decorations, brightly painted, as typical of other pre-Columbian structures. Such elaboration does not seem to conform with the sober and refined spirit of the Classic Maya. Perhaps this resulted from the particular social and political makeup of these cities where frequently the palaces and residences—that is, dwellings of man—were more important than temples dedicated to gods.

The Rain God Chac

Kabah is sometimes referred to as a kind of satellite city of Uxmal and is often regarded as being of less importance when, in actuality, its central area is even larger than that of Uxmal. The area is approximately 4,000 feet from east to west and 3,000 feet from north to south. The city is divided almost in half by the causeway that passes through it. On each side of the causeway there are four main groups of buildings. Unfortunately, the four groups on the western side of the causeway have never been cleared or restored which is one reason that Kabah seems to be a smaller and less important site than Uxmal.

The buildings on the east of the causeway have been cleared and somewhat restored. The two main groups, which are closest to the causeway, consist of a small quadrangle group and a temple plaza group containing the largest pyramid of the entire site. East of these two groups and across a plaza, now cut by the modern Mérida-Campeche Highway, are the other two main groups in the eastern half of the city. These are the best preserved buildings at Kabah and

Codz Pop, The Palace of the Masks, Kabah

Corbelled arch at Kabah which stands at the end of an ancient Mayan road.

consist of the Codz Pop, and just northeast of the Codz Pop a group of buildings that form a quadrangle but whose style is characteristic of Palace groups, having parallel ranges of rooms with doorways on either side of the long facades. Surrounding these structures on three sides are a second set of buildings on lower terraces. It has not been determined whether this group served as a palace or should be classified as a quadrangle. East of this complex, at the far edge of the map, lie two minor groups. Both consist of palace-type buildings. Their distance from the rest of the complexes may indicate that their function was essentially different from that of the rest of the buildings.

South of the entire complex, but connected to it by the causeway, is a fairly good-sized pyramid. Although it is connected to the rest of the city by the causeway, it is essentially quite isolated and could represent the central point of a smaller suburban area.

Uxmal (OOS-mahl)

One of the largest and most beautiful archaeological zones in America, Uxmal is located 47 miles south of Merida on Highway 261. Originally called "Oxmal" by the Maya, it means "thrice built." It covers several hundred acres and, at one time, there may have been more than a million people living there. It is of the same time and tradition as Kabah, Sayil, and Labna, being in the late Classic period (c. A.D. 900); however, many buildings have been found representing the Classic Mayan period (A.D. 300 to A.D. 900). While most of the buildings were constructed during the Classic Mayan period, the Toltec influence is seen by extensive building from the Mayan-Toltec period (late Classic).

The most prominent and well-known structure is the Temple of the Magician, also known as the House of the Dwarf, and the Pyramid of the Sorcerer, named because of a legend of a dwarf who was a magician who supposedly lived there. Rising to 125 feet, the temple-pyramid immediately greets the visitor to the area. The building can be climbed using an extremely steep stairway of 118 steps to the top. A safety chain is available for security. The pyramid is shaped somewhat elliptically at the base with rounded sides and with three terraced areas and a worship building on top. It has undergone various periods of construction from which five different temples have been defined. Four temples lie underneath, one inside the other. The present temple was the last one constructed.

Next to the pyramid is the Nunnery, erroneously named by the Spaniards because it reminded them of a convent. The most interesting way to enter this section is through a beautiful Mayan

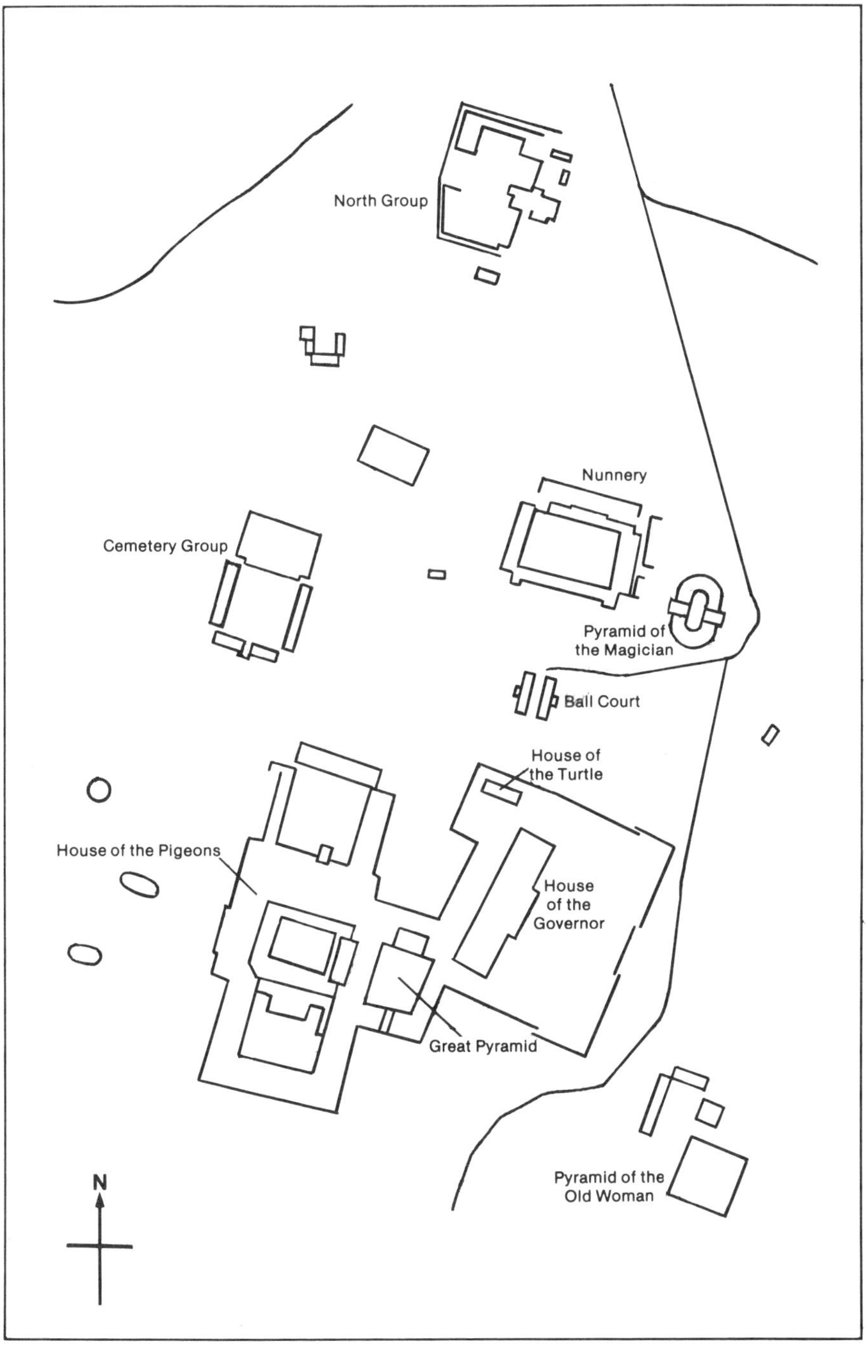
North Group
Nunnery
Cemetery Group
Pyramid of the Magician
Ball Court
House of the Turtle
House of the Pigeons
House of the Governor
Great Pyramid
Pyramid of the Old Woman
N

Uxmal

The Nunnery, Uxmal

Corbelled Arch of the Governor's Palace, Uxmal

Temple of the Magician, Uxmal

archway from the south which gives access to the inner court. On the buildings surrounding the courtyard are some of the finest examples of Maya architecture and lapidary art. One of these buildings is called the Temple of Venus because of a motif on its frieze that has been associated with this particular planet. Masks of the rain god Chac, with the curly nose, mounted one above another, ornament the front of the Nunnery. Stones cut precisely from an extraordinarily beautiful mosaic pattern become the upper part of the wall facing the Nunnery's four-sided patio. Slender columns are part of the decor on the lower part of the wall, while grillwork mosaics form the design on the upper wall. The Nunnery has a cloister effect with its numerous individual rooms. Only a base now remains of a statue of a large jaguar that stood in the center of the court which measures 215 feet by 150 feet.

The beautiful Governor's Palace, 600 feet long by 500 feet wide and 40 feet high, has a terraced effect. As with all the buildings in Uxmal, the governor's palace is built of white coral limestone. The carving in the stone on the facade of the upper part of the front of the building is superb. Approximately 20,000 individual stones, each weighing 55 to 175 pounds, were used in its construction. Another section of the building features stepped terraces and is 400 feet long, 90 feet wide, and 23 feet high. The third section is 320 feet long, 40 feet wide, and 26 feet high. Roofed hallways with high vaults connect the three sections.

The House of Turtles, a few feet northwest of the Governor's Palace, has a simple design with a facade similar to classical Greek architecture. It derives its name from the turtles carved in the lintels of the cornice.

The archaeological city of Uxmal, thrice built, is considered one of the most successful architectural achievements of the Mayan civilization. The inhabitants made use of cisterns to catch rain water for drinking and extensive culinary purposes. This region does not have water holes, so rainwater was looked upon with great reverence.

A small ball court still remains at Uxmal. It had several long row-like buildings that were probably used as grandstands.

Mérida to Puerto Juarez (Highway 180, 202 miles)

The bustling city of Mérida is the hub of eastern Mexico and the Yucatán Peninsula. At the turn of the century the sale of henequen—fiber used to make rope—made many people there rich. The city claimed there were more millionaires per capita in Mérida than in any other place. They built fabulous homes and lived in high style.

The zocalo or Plaza de Independencia is the center of town. It is the site of a great Mayan temple and pyramid. The Franciscan Church of the Tercera Orden is built largely from the rubble taken from Mayan ceremonial buildings. Inside the cathedral is an interesting panoramic painting, depicting a formal visit made by Tutul Xiu (shee-oo) the Mayan ruler of Mani, to the conquistador Montejo.

Before leaving Mérida for Chichén Itzá and points east, take a quick trip north if you can. The port of Progreso lies a few kilometers away, on Highway 261. About ten miles out of Mérida, on the right, will be a road to the archaeological zone of Dzibulchaltún, three miles off the road, one of the oldest continuously occupied settlements in the Americas.

Dzibilchaltún (See-beel-chal-TOON)

Close to the ocean, north of the city of Mérida, Yucatán, Mexico, lie the ruins of Dzibilchaltún. E. Wyllys Andrews began excavating the ruins in about 1956. The ruins represent the largest known Mayan city covering approximately 50 square kilometers with 20 square kilometers of it being mapped in detail as the central area. The levels of occupation indicate that the earliest habitation could have been near 2000 B.C., and it appears to have been continuously inhabited until the Spanish conquest. The bulk of the exposed ruins, however, date from the Classic period (A.D. 300 to A.D. 900). These dates correlate well within the Book of Mormon time frame.

While civilizations in nearby Chichén Itzá, Uxmal, etc., came and went, life went on at Dzibilchaltún, or "Where There Is Writing on Flat Rocks."

Dzibilchatún is believed to have been a trade center for a vast area. Discarded and broken pottery, in a sequence of ceramics covering several thousand years, has been found in the foundations and walls. Excavation of a large well, or cenote, in the center of the area has unearthed pottery from several phases of Mayan civilization. Decorative motifs and murals in stucco adorn the walls. The city was built around plazas and patios, and stelae dot the city ruins. Connecting various plazas are great causeways similar to other Mayan sites in that along its length it is marked by stelae with sculptured figures and hieroglyphic inscriptions.

Tradition has it that the entire city was submerged when the big lake of Boca Paila suddenly formed. The city, which was the center of a populous urban area in the Classic period, had sustained the longest known continuous habitation of any Mayan city (2000 to

3000 years). It was a main trade center of the entire area and possibly with cities of other empires as well.

One of the most interesting of the ruins at Dzibilchaltún is the pyramid-temple structure called the Temple of the Seven Dolls. This temple dates from approximately A.D. 500 and, although it follows the basic form of Mayan pyramid temples in having the substructure, which consists of a stepped pyramid, the temple with a few interior rooms and the roof comb, the details of these elements vary considerably from those found at the other Mayan sites.

Most Mayan temples consist of a small structure built atop a pyramid with two or three vaulted rooms, sometimes side by side and sometimes one behind the other. Almost always the doors leading to these rooms are found on one side of the temple only. The Temple of the Seven dolls, however, has an entrance on each side. The interior room also has entrances on all four sides. But perhaps the most interesting parts of this structure are the two small openings in the outer walls of the temple. They resemble what we would, today, call windows. This kind of opening is entirely unknown at any other Mayan site dating from the same period of time.

Temple of the Seven Dolls, Dzibilchaltún

Dzibilchaltún

The roof combs on most Mayan temples consist of a wall-like structure, usually parallel to the front of the building which has been pierced so as to give it a lacy effect. The roof comb atop the Temple of the Seven Dolls, however, is built so as to face all four sides of the temple and thus forms a square, or a small room, on top of the temple and narrows toward the top somewhat resembling a small, truncated pyramid. The large pyramid upon which the temple rests is also somewhat different. It has stairs leading to the top on all four sides, an effect somewhat rare in Mayan architecture.

Along Highway 180, after leaving Mérida, are the small ruins of Izamal and the major zone of Chichén Itzá. The road to Izamal is about 42 miles east of Mérida, and the ruin is 15 miles north of the highway. The substructure of the pyramid rises to 40 feet and is 200 yards long at each side of the base. This was once a sacred city of the Itzas, but the Spaniards covered part of the ruin with a church-monastery in the late 1500s. The town is built all around the pyramid which is covered with vegetation and difficult to see.

After returning to Highway 180, continue on to Chichén Itzá about 30 miles east. For this famous zone, plan on several hours for sightseeing. In winter and summer the Yucatán Peninsula is warm, so take it easy. From Chichén Itzá to Puerto Juárez and the coast is about 125 miles.

Chichén Itzá (Chee-CHAIN-ee-TSAH)

By far the most well-known of the ruins in Mesoamerica, Chichén Itzá arises in the plains of Yucatán about 75 miles east of Mérida. The majestic Temple of Kukulcan, also known as El Castillo, is probably the most photographed and recognized site in Mexico.

"Chi" means "mouth" in Maya, "Chen" means "waterwell," while "Itza" was the name of a group that once inhabited the place. Therefore, the composition of the three words would signify "On the mouth of the well of the Itzá," meaning "The location of the city by the well." A cenote (sacred well) is the focal point of the ceremonial center there.

The archaeological zone of Chichén Itzá covers approximately four square miles and is divided into three sections—the Northern, Central, and Southern. The latter is called "Old Chichén," and is made up of various groups of buildings located at different distances from one another. They are, for the most part, in ruins. The Central Group is the oldest and the Northern Group is the newest.

Temple of Kukulcan, or El Castillo, Chichén Itzá

The Sacred Well (cenote) at Chichén Itzá

Chichén was occupied twice. The Itzás, a Mayan group, occupied it from about the fourth century A.D. to around A.D. 900. Many of the buildings are distinctly Mayan. It was abandoned for a while, then the Toltecs left their home in Tula (north of Mexico City) and settled on the remains of the complex. It is said they were led by Ce Acatl Topiltzin Quetzalcoatl, King of Tula and usurper of the attributes of the white god Quetzalcoatl (*see* Tula).

The Mayas had been peaceful and studious, but the Toltecs were a warlike group. When they came in, they founded the northern section and life was centered around the sacred well, their sacrificial repository. This second occupation was between A.D. 975 and A.D. 1200. This is called the Toltec period. They worshiped the god Quetzalcoatl, but here the name was changed to the Mayan name Kukulcan which had the meaning of the great Fair God who has attributes similar to those of Jesus Christ.

The entrance of Chichén is in the northern section where the Temple of Kukulcan is an impressive sight. This four-sided pyramid rises to a height of about 80 feet. It is comprised of two different constructions both of which belong to the Toltec period. The outer

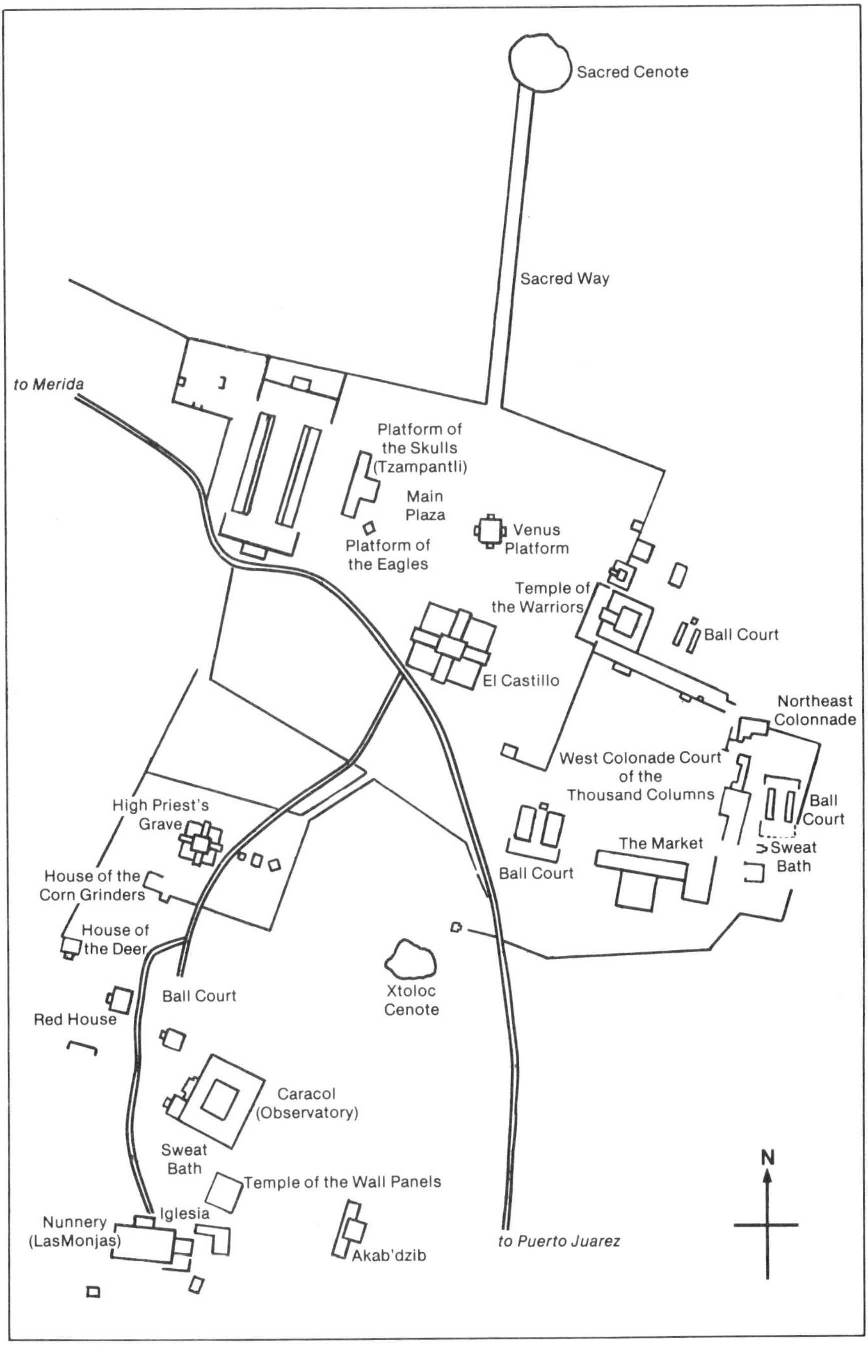

Chichén Itzá

pyramid actually sits over another smaller structure of the same shape. It consists of nine superimposed platforms which decrease in size with the elevation of the pyramid. A stairway goes up each side over the platforms, and at the base of each balustrade of the stairway there are figures of huge serpent heads, representing Kukulcan.

This pyramid may have represented a calendar of the Mayas since the stairways consist of 91 steps on each side which, multiplied, equals 364. At the summit there is a square edifice, making a total of 365. The sides face each direction, and some say they also represent the seasons of the year.

The Temple of Kukulcan is an excellent example of just how advanced the ancient Mayan really were in astronomical observations. As is true of various structures among the Maya and other Mesoamerican cultures, the pyramid is set at a seventeen-degree angle off magnetic north. The phenomenon brought about by the shadows on the day of equinox makes the reason for the offset clear. It has been discovered that from 5 p.m. to sunset, on March 21 and September 22, the corners of the superimposed platforms on the northeast project, in succession, making shadows on the rim of the balustrade of the stairs on the northern side in seven isosceles triangles, with the last forming the neck of the enormous serpent's head. This head rests on the base of the balustrade. As the sun slowly set it gave the impression of an undulating line of triangles which represented the body of the serpent, as if the snake were moving. This meant, anciently (and still means to the Mayans today) that the time to plant their crops has arrived.

The inner pyramid of Kukulcan was found in 1931. At the base of one of the stairways of the inner pyramid was found a stone box. It contained human bones, two turquoise mosaics, two flint daggers, and a priceless necklace made of many pieces of jade of various sizes. The jade mosaics were taken to the anthropological museum in Mérida, the flint daggers and the necklace to the museum, and the stone box was left on the outside of the pyramid where it can be seen today.

According to the description, the stone box Joseph Smith found containing the golden plates was not too different from this box at Chichén. This one is located near the entrance to the stairs of the inner pyramid that leads to the summit of the structure. At this summit there are two chambers. In the first chamber is a reclining idol "chacmool" (another of these idols is on the Temple of the Warriors). In the second chamber there is a beautiful jaguar, about two and three-fourths feet high, made from a single piece of stone

The Jaded Jaguar inside El Castillo, Chichén Itzá

painted red, with glaring eyes and 72 spots made of jade, menacing white stone teeth and a jade-incrusted tail.

Entrance to this inner pyramid is possible only during certain hours. It is reached after a very steep climb up a small passageway and the air is thin. Caution should be observed. Discomfort is ignored, however, once the jaguar is in sight.

Next to the pyramid is the complex of the Temple of the Warriors. Hundreds of columns representing plumed warriors were used to hold up the roof. On top of the stairway, between two massive stone snakes, reclines probably the most photographed man in the Americas. He is the "chacmool" (the word comes from the Mayan words for "claw" and "red"), a receptacle for receiving the hearts of sacrificial victims.

The cenote (well) is a short walk away. From the well the bones of young humans who were sacrificed to the gods have been recovered.

The cenote (well) is a short walk away. From the well the bones of young humans who were sacrificed to the gods have been recovered. It has also yielded thousands of artifacts, jewelry pottery, and other valuable items. Amazingly, some came from as far away as Panama.

The largest ball court in Mesoamerica is located in the Northern Zone of Chichén Itzá. The acoustics are so good that a normal-toned voice can be heard throughout the playing field. From under the stone rings on each side one can hear some twelve echos when the hands are clapped. Bearded figures are found in the carved scenes on each side of the court on the face of the low platforms.

The magnificent El Caracol, or the Observatory, is in the Southern Zone of Chichén. It is pure Maya architecture and one of the most beautiful and important buildings in the ruin. Here the serpents have scales while the serpents of the Toltecs were plumed.

The Temple of the Warriors, Chichén Itzá

El Carocol (The Snail) Observatory, Chichén Itzá

The observatory derived its name from its shape and from the fact that at sunset, between 5:00 and 5:30 p.m. on the days of the equinox, the left outside edge of the window in the dome reflects on the right interior edge of the same window. This can be observed by a person standing within the tower.

The name "caracol," meaning "snail," comes from a narrow spiral staircase in the center part of the dome built in the form of a snail.

South of the observatory is a small building, the Temple of the Wall Panels (or plaques). On one wall is carved a figure of an animal that, according to Milton R. Hunter, could be a horse. If so, this is puzzling since there were no horses in the New World when the Spaniards came. The Book of Mormon refers to horses frequently.

Further south is the Nunnery. In the rear of this building is another building that has interesting hieroglyphics on the lintel above the door.

Mayan roads (sacbe) are numerous throughout Yucatán, and some of them connect Chichén Itzá with other centers and with the seacoast. The name is derived from two Mayan words, "sac," meaning "white," and "be," meaning "road." The Maya surfaced their roads with a white earth called "sascab."

The Nunnery at Chichén Itzá

Mayan Road (Sacbe)

Stone Ring for Ancient Ball Game, Chichén Itzá

The Mayan and Toltec civilizations who once used these structures of Chichén Itzá left abruptly and mysteriously. However, the contributions of the people who inhabited this area are numerous and the study of their civilizations fascinating.

Puerto Juárez to Chetumal (Highway 307, 240 miles)

Now it is play and relaxing time. Isla Mujeres, Cancun and Isla Cozumel are delightful on the clear, blue-green Caribbean Sea.

From Cancun, which has some very expensive hotels, there is a sightseeing boat to Isla Mujeres for a visit of a few hours. There is a car ferry from Puerto Juárez which takes about half an hour and runs several times a day. The hotels are fair, and there may be facilities for self-contained RVs. Only 90 miles from Cuba, the little island is the very tip of Mexico. It used to be an outpost for pirates. The Spaniards named the island "island of women" because of the idols of female form found by the little Mayan building on the south end of the island. It is an interesting little place in which to spend time wandering around the dock and village.

All along this coast scuba diving, fishing, sailing, and sunning are favorite sports.

The unique ruins of Tulúm are 74 miles south along the coast road 307. Just south of Tulúm is a new paved road leading to Cobá, 25 miles inland. Return to 307 along the same road to continue on to Chetumal, about 120 miles south of Tulúm.

Tulúm

Not considered one of the major ruins—but certainly the most beautifully situated—is the walled city of Tulúm. A 25-foot high Castillo is perched on a 40-foot cliff overlooking the clear, blue-green Caribbean Sea. The waves of the sea eternally dash against the large rocks that have tumbled from the cliff into the water. It was first seen by Europeans when a Spanish expedition, led by Juan de Grijalva, sailed along the coast in the sixteenth century. The site had been abandoned and overgrown with brush. Later, in 1848, John L. Stephens and Frederick Catherwood cleared and explored the ruins.

From pottery sherds, there is evidence of occupation during the Classic period (A.D. 300 to 900). The city was walled on three sides with the fourth side protected by the sea. Originally the walls were 35 feet thick and 30 feet high with corner blockhouses. The five entrances, only three feet wide, led into the 16-acre site. According to archaeologist Michael Coe, probably no more than five or six hundred people lived there. The city was probably an important

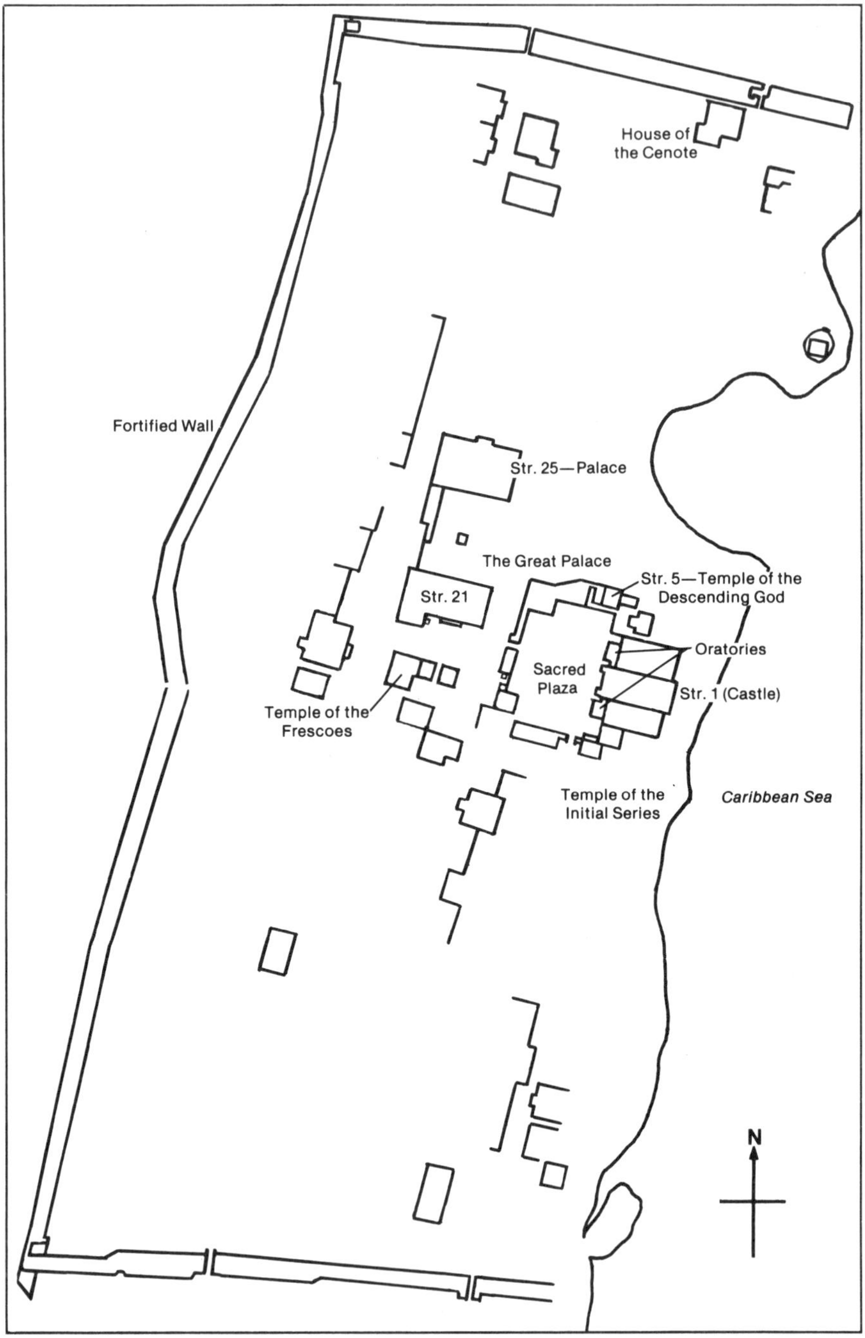
House of
the Cenote
Fortified Wall
Str. 25—Palace
The Great Palace
Str. 5—Temple of the
Descending God
Str. 21
Oratories
Sacred
Plaza
Str. 1 (Castle)
Temple of the
Frescoes
Temple of the
Initial Series
Caribbean Sea
N

Tulúm

trading center where merchants could route goods from the Caribbean to the Petén and Usumacinta regions of Guatemala and Mexico. The town was also important for intercoastal trade.

Besides the Castillo (the Spaniards seemed to have named the largest structure in every ancient site a "castle"), the most interesting and principal structure is Temple Number Five. This is also known as the Temple of the Descending or Diving God because of a large figure in a headlong position over the main entrance. This motif is used in other buildings at Tulúm, as well as on structures at Sayil and El Tajın.

Descending gods have been used consistently since Classic times all over Mesoamerica. Each researcher has his own idea of what "god" means, but only LDS researchers recognize the fact that, when Christ appeared to the people on the American continent, He descended from the sky.

Another interesting building is the Temple of the Frescoes where colorful murals are visible. On one corner is a giant face of a god with (what used to be) a jade bead in his mouth. Jade and the color green were ancient symbols of the White God Quetzalcoatl, and Hazel Davala, a guide at Tulúm, said that a jade bead in the mouth was the symbol of the resurrection. Mrs. Davala also said that the little square building near the Temple of the Frescoes was an astronomical structure that had a small hole in it placed so that the sun shines through, every April 6th, onto a short column structure in the center of the building. She called the building "The Season's Dial Building," and there were similar holes in buildings in Uxmal, Becal (on the Yucatán side of the Gulf of Mexico), Tajín (across the Gulf of Mexico), and Talpa (on the Pacific side of Mexico), all on a straight line across Mexico from east to west.

Another hole in the Castillo allows the sun to shine in on the days of the equinox. There are plumed-serpent columns on the Castillo, also, representative of Quetzalcoatl.

Cobá

A hub of series of roads (more than sixteen have been found), Cobá is located south of Tulúm, 47 kilometers off Highway 307. The road that connected Cobá with a town known as Yaxuna, a few miles from Chichén Itzá, was a broad causeway. The longest in the ancient Maya area, it stretched for 62 and a half miles, with an average width of 8 feet. It averaged 2 feet in height, crossing swamps at an elevation of as much as 8 feet. Large boulders, methodically integrated with small stones, formed the construction of the road.

It was bound together with a kind of cement. The surface, which was of cement, is now almost completely destroyed.

Nestled in the jungle, Cobá was one of the largest cities in northwestern Yucatán during the Classic period. It was built between two lakes and contained clusters of inter-related buildings. A small pyramid (or temple) has the traditional steps to the top and tunnels in the base.

Chetumal is the capital of the state of Quintana Roo. It is a port town with a large, busy harbor that ships products of the peninsula such as chicle (for chewing gum), tobacco, bananas, and precious hardwoods. (Many of the ruins in the southern Mexico-Belize-Guatemala area were discovered by men looking for chicle trees, bananas, and hardwood. Companies such as United Fruit Company have given financial aid to explore and restore the sights.)

This is the take-off point for trips to Belize (just across the river). If time permits, a drive down to the Mayan ruin of Altun Ha in Belize (formerly British Honduras) is a unique experience.

If you are tired of Mexican music on your radio by now, you will be happy to listen to an English-speaking station from Belize City while driving near Chetumal.

Altun Ha

This is a ceremonial-habitation complex located in the country of Belize. It lies in the jungle about 70 miles south of the Mexican border, near Chetumal, and is about 30 miles from Belize City. There is only one road into the country.

It was an active center of economic, ceremonial, and political activity during the Classic period (A.D. 150 to 900). The importance of Altun Ha within the Maya arises from its control over maritime trade and resources. As compensation for this privilege, the lords of Altun Ha exacted a tremendous amount of imports from highland Guatemala and from as far as Central Mexico. Among these was the largest carved jade item—a head in representation of the Sun God Ahua—ever to be found in the Maya area.

The main ceremonial center features two large plazas surrounded by temples and priestly residences constructed from Pre-Classic (300 B.C. to A.D. 150) times. These dates indicate it was occupied and flourishing during Book of Mormon times.

Belize has pre-Columbian ruins abounding all through it. One of these sites is called *Lamani* and, according to the Belize guidebook, it is the only site in Belize whose present name was given to it by its original Maya inhabitants. The names of other pre-Columbian sites were given to them by the later cultures or by the Spaniards.

The ceremonial complex there was in use from Pre-Classic to Post-Classic times (2000 B.C. to A.D. 1540).

Chetumal to Escarcega (Highway 186, 162 miles)

This is the long, straight stretch of road which completes the circle of the Yucatán.

Continue west on Highway 186 until you reach the desired turn-off to go to Oaxaca.

Escarcega to Oaxaca

To cross the Isthmus of Tehuantepec to reach the road to Oaxaca, take the road south from Palenque to San Cristobal de las Casas, Highway 195 to Chiapa de Corzo, or Highway 185 from Minatitlán to Highway 200, and turn north.

Near the city of Oaxaca are the small but artistic ruins of Dainzu, Mitla, and Yagul, and the major archaeological zone of Monte Albán. The three small ones are along the highway, south of town, but Monte Albán is just out of town a little way on a high, leveled hill. There are signs directing the visitor to the area.

Dainzú

Dainzú is located near Tlacolula, Mexico, on the road to Mitla, Highway 190. Carvings at the site date from as far back as 700 B.C. and are similar to the Danzante figures of Monte Albán. It is the only other site known that has figures similar to those of Monte Albán.

Dainzú has only partially been restored as excavation was just recently begun there. The site is quite extensive with plazas, courtyards, burial chambers, pyramids, and ball courts. The ball court has been partially restored and is quite similar to the one at Monte Albán, although it would appear, from the carvings of ball players on the walls, that the game was played differently here than at other sites. Most players wore masks and helmets and in the carvings these can be seen as well as the strings used to hold them on. Many of the players also carry a ball in their hands. The balls are small and must have been extremely hard as the players wore leg and arm protectors as well as masks and helmets. It is probable that the balls were made of hard rubber because rubber is indigenous to the area.

Structure A, located above the main plaza, is often referred to as "the pyramid of the ball players" because this is where the carvings mentioned above are located. On top of this structure is a tomb.

Much new information can be expected as the excavation of Dainzú continues.

Mitla (MEET-la)

This remarkable ruin, covering an area of 1,640 feet from north to south and 948 feet from east to west, is located about 25 miles southeast of Oaxaca on Highway 190. It is thought that the Zapotec culture of Monte Albán retreated to this area and settled here. In the Zapotec language, Mitla is called "Yoo-paa," or "Place of the Dead."

Mitla is unique in that, instead of large temple pyramids, there are several sprawling, lower buildings with flat roofs and courtyards. There are five separate complexes. The church group and the palace group are the best known. The palace group is where the Hall of Columns and the Patio of the Tombs are located. Some archaeologists believe that these structures were built just prior to the Spanish conquest.

The most intriguing architectural achievements are the angular mosaics of protruding stones set in rhythmic repetition of geometric designs. It has been estimated that 130,000 individually cut stones were made to produce these beautiful mosaic patterns. No mortar was used between the pores, and the joints are barely visible with the patterns blending flawlessly. The "false mosaic" was also incorporated for use at Mitla: large, solid stones needed for lintels over doorways, etc., carved to look like true mosaics made up of smaller cut stones.

Hall of Pillars at Mitla

Mosiac Wall Patterns at Mitla

In certain places these stones were painted and even today, in what is now known as "the church group," a series of chambers exist where the mosaic stones were painted: the projecting stones in white and the background stones in a deep red. The other walls and floor were also painted deep red. One observer has referred to these mosaics as "petrified weaving." Some interior walls contrasted this design by displaying beautifully painted frescoes.

The people of Mitla believed in an afterlife, and great care was taken in tomb construction such as the one found in the form of a large cross beneath the level of the pyramid floor. Sometimes a tomb contained only one body, but more often a tomb was a collective grave.

Mitla represented a mixture of Zapotec and Mixteca-Puebla cultures. The people inherited much from their ancestors. However, they did innovate that which had come down to them and thus they developed hieroglyphic writing, astronomy, mathematics, a calendrical system, and many realistic art pieces in painting, bas-reliefs, architecture, corbelled vaulting, and tower roofing on temples. They created beautiful turquoise mosaics, miniature painted codices, and fine gold work.

Yagul (Ya-gool)

On Highway 190, south of Oaxaca in the valley of Oaxaca on a raised platform area, lies the restored ruin of Yagul. There are various levels on this hillside site, and the largest building (Palace of Six Patios) is a huge structure with more than thirty rooms most of which are ranged around these patios.

The whole unit has only one entrance which leads into a long hallway that divides it into two unequal parts. In the western section are four patios; in the eastern section are two which are better constructed and more elaborate. As at Mitla, portions of the exterior walls were covered by stone mosaics, but these have disappeared. Explorations have recovered but few of the remains, possibly because stone from this ancient city was used to build part of the modern town of Tlacolula, its neighbor. Many of the walls are still covered with the original red plaster.

On a lower level is another large unit comprising the Sala del Consejo (Assembly Hall), a vast room similar to that at the entrance to the main palace at Mitla but without the monolithic columns. On this level are other civic buildings, the ball court, and other patios surrounded by large rooms. Only a tall pyramid, now in very bad condition, suggests that a temple once stood here. Much higher up is the fortress, formed in part by natural rocks and in part by stone walls.

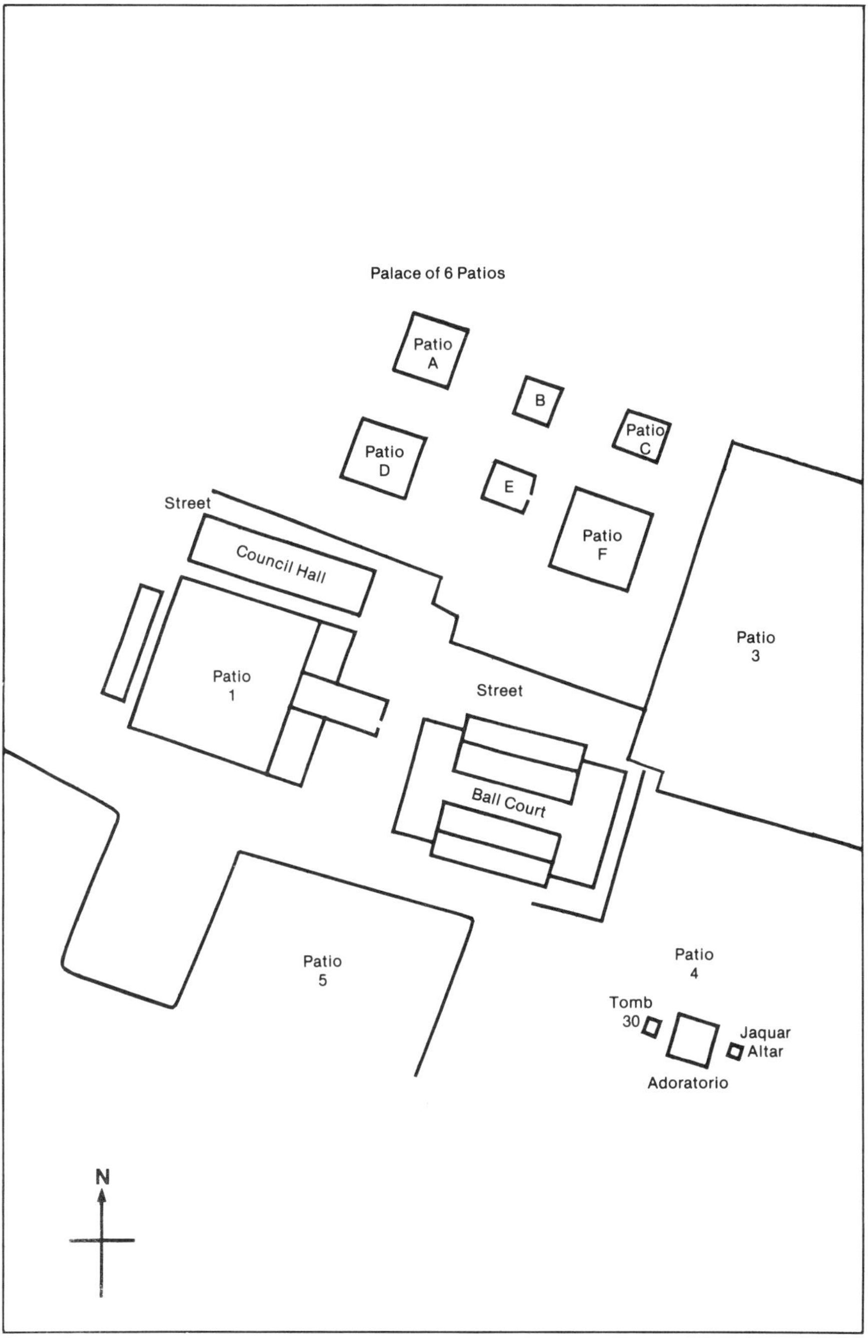
Palace of 6 Patios
Patio A
B
Patio C
Patio D
E
Patio F
Street
Council Hall
Patio 1
Street
Patio 3
Ball Court
Patio 5
Patio 4
Tomb 30
Jaquar Altar
Adoratorio
N

Yagul

Yagul

This ruin did not emphasize the religious motif. There are indications that it was a military or administrative unit. From any part of this ruin one has a panoramic view of the beautiful valley of Oaxaca. This may have been why Yagul was built in the hills—as a fortress and protection for the cities below.

Monte Albán (MOAN-tay Awl-BAWN)

The ceremonial center of Monte Albán is one of the most famous archaeological sites of pre-Columbian ruins. Six miles west of Oaxaca City, this site is perched high on a man-leveled hill 6500 feet above sea level with a panoramic view of all possible approaches. This position suggests that Monte Albán may have been, originally, a defensive stronghold.

No two researchers agree on the dates of Monte Albán (Sacred Mountain or White Mountain), but all agree that it was one of the oldest centers in Mexico. Its occupation continued from the early Pre-Classic period—perhaps as early as 1000 B.C.—until the coming of the Spaniards in 1522. [15]

During this time five cultures dominated the area. The ancient citizens of these eras were not without their brilliant engineers

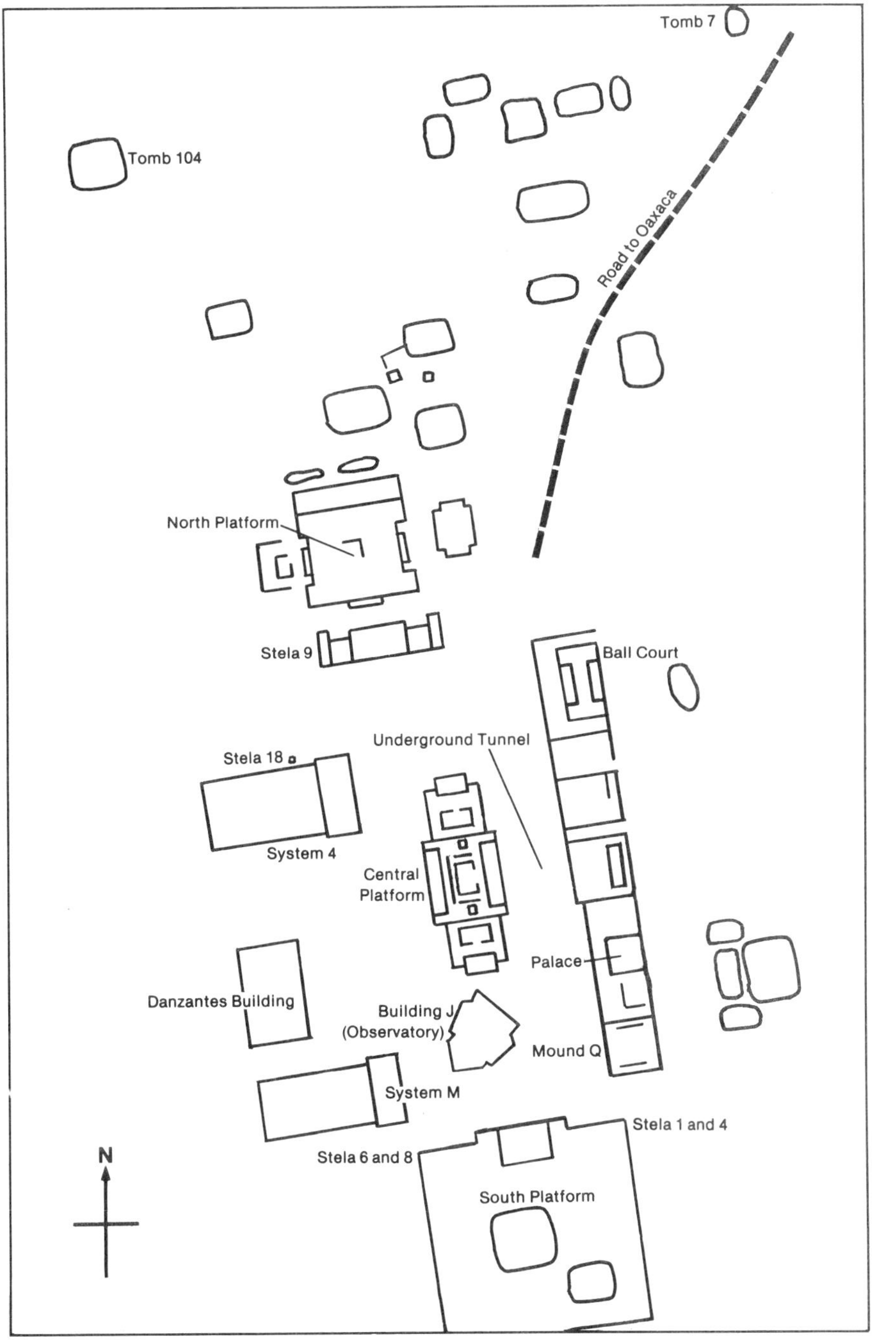
Tomb 7
Tomb 104
Road to Oaxaca
North Platform
Stela 9
Ball Court
Underground Tunnel
Stela 18
System 4
Central Platform
Palace
Danzantes Building
Building J (Observatory)
Mound Q
System M
Stela 1 and 4
Stela 6 and 8
South Platform
N

Monte Albán

because the top of the entire hill was scraped off and leveled in preparation for a magnificent complex of religious temples and buildings which occupy an area a mile long and a quarter-of-a-mile wide. Some of the structures were built over others. One of the most imposing houses of worship is the massive temple to the north of the quadrangle which contains crumbling circular pillars. Wide, majestic steps lead to the summit and are covered with white stucco. This stairway represents three separate periods of construction and it is believed to be the widest temple entrance in all America.

No one knows who the first settlers were, but the carvings in an edifice that has been given the name "Temple de los Danzantes," or "Temple of the Dancers," are in Olmec style. Numerous bas-relief figures, carved on large stone slabs and thought to resemble dancers, have been found in this building. Most recently, speculation has suggested that certain anatomical sections of this carving refer to the human body. It is thought that this could be part of a medical school. This period is known as Monte Albán I.

The date for the beginning of Monte Albán II differs, but it is estimated to be around 200 B.C. to the year 1 when a group of people from the Chiapas Highlands entered.

This second group could be either the Mulekites or the Nephites, according to some BYU researchers, depending on what date is ascertained. Their studies suggest that the Mexican state of Chiapas

Monte Albán

was the scene of the Nephites and the Land Southward, and the Oaxaca Valley in between with the Land Northward and the Isthmus of Tehuantepec ("narrow neck of land").

The date of 55 B.C., when the Nephites began a number of migrations to the "land northward," coincides with the time the Chiapa Highlanders moved into Monte Albán if the latter part of the 200 B.C. to 1 B.C. time span is accepted. However:

> If the earlier (200 B.C.) time frame is used then the bearers of the new culture were probably Mulekites from Chiapa de Corzo. In this latter case the movement was not described directly in the Book of Mormon.[16]

Mount "J," also called the Observatory, was constructed during this period. An arched tunnel cuts across the building and is open at the top. For this reason it is called "The Observatory" on the assumption that the openings were used to make astral computations. (This is only conjecture.) There are glyphs—bas-reliefs called "danzantes" on the structure that have been interpreted by some investigators to mean that the building was dedicated as a triumphal record of conquest.

Monte Albán was well-positioned for a military capital. Secluded on a high, leveled hill, it is reminiscent of Megiddo and Masada, fortresses in Israel. No weapons or military evidences have been uncovered as yet, however. Cold is unknown in this area, and during the summer the heat is not excessive.

The Zapotecs entered the site for Monte Albán III about the beginning of the Christian era. During this time the greatest structures were built. The influence of the city was at its zenith, its arts and designs coming into their finest flowering and with creative efforts at their peak. The Zapotecs still inhabit much of the valley of Oaxaca. On market day, they and the Mixtecs come into town to sell their handmade products such as pottery, shawls, and baskets. Many objects are of a beauty unequalled elsewhere in Mexico.

Monte Albán IV runs from approximately A.D. 1000 until around A.D. 1250; a time when the site stopped being used for the living and became a burial ground for the dead. Over 150 tombs have been uncovered, some painted with brilliant murals. One of the buildings to the west of the quadrangle contained the tomb of a very important personage. The contents of the tomb are on display at the Mexican National Museum of Anthropology in Mexico City.

The last period—Monte Albán V—came when the Mixtecs moved in from the Cholula-Puebla area. The Aztecs arrived a short time before the Spanish conquerors arrived in about 1522.

Ball Field at Monte Albán

One of the wonders of the site is that there is no water supply. Every drop had to be carried up from the valley below and stored in special urns.

Almost all of the pre-Columbian ruins in Mexico were constructed with a cement-like substance and painted in brilliant colors. Monte Albán was no exception. The surfaces were painted with bright blues, reds, greens, and yellows, and had figures of deities, stylized animals and gods, heavenly bodies, and battle scenes, all portrayed in these vivid colors.

Oaxaca to Mexico City (Highway 190)

For the return trip from Oaxaca to Mexico City, Highway 190 is the road to take. Some of it goes through mountain ranges, but it is a good, fast road.

This highway takes you to a junction at Izucar de Matamoros where you can continue through on 190 to Puebla (and Cholula if you have missed that ruin), or you can take Highway 160 to Cuautla. Out of Cuautla you can either take the fast toll on in to Mexico, or go to the charming city of Cuernavaca. If you have missed the ruins of Xochicalco 28 miles south of Cuernavaca, be sure to see them now.

Bienvenidos a Mexico. Welcome back to Mexico City. We hope your journey has been *magnifico*!

CHAPTER FOUR

Guatemala and Copan, Honduras

About the Country

You know you are in Guatemala when you hear the marimba bands! When you encounter a group of talented musicians playing several of these lovely sounding instruments in the parks, restaurants, nightclubs or for fiestas it is hard to break away. The melodious marimba was invented by the Mayans and it is a popular instrument throughout Guatemala.

There are two ways to get to Guatemala from Mexico. The northern route is Mexico Highway 190 which becomes CA 1, in Guatemala, at Ciudad Cuauhtemoc. This is a mountainous but beautiful highway which is near several important archaeological sites.

The southern route is Highway 200 at Tapachula, Mexico, which becomes Guatemala Highway CA 2 at Talisman. You can also cross the border at Ciudad Hidalgo but Talisman is a larger port of entry. This is a fast, easy road to drive but there is little scenery.

The dense Petén jungle in northern Guatemala prevents road construction so the number of entrances to the country are limited.

There are many guided tours into Guatemala, and tours to points of interest in the country. Tours may be the best way to visit the country for most people.

Life in Guatemala is determined by where one lives—in the city, a small town, or a village. Guatemala City is a modern, progressive cosmopolitan metropolis, the largest capital in Central America. The hospitable people enjoy the pleasant, spring-like climate the 500-foot elevation affords them year round. Village life is sometimes primitive and passive.

Since about two-thirds of Guatemala is mountainous and volcanic, the inhabitants learn to live (if that is possible) with the tremorous terrain.

It is interesting for the visitor to Guatemala to see how three cultures—ancient Indian, Colonial Spanish, and modern—live side by side and form a unique combination of the old and new. In the Petén—a dense rain forest in the Guatemalan highlands—live the Maya Indians just as they have for centuries. They make up almost one-half of the six million population of the country. The influence of the Spanish conquerors is found in the religion, culture, and architecture of the country, especially in the town of Antigua which was originally the capital of Guatemala. An earthquake in 1773 partly destroyed Antigua and the capital was moved to Guatemala City which has adopted the attributes and architecture of modern cities throughout the world. It is a lovely town, however, with broad avenues decorated with fountains and statues.

Guatemala is an extremely beautiful country. Its boundaries extend from the Gulf of Mexico to the Caribbean Sea, and there are flowering jungles and mountain lakes.

Besides being an absolutely beautiful scenic wonder and tourist attraction, one of these lakes (Atitlán, off Highways CA 1 and RN 1 between Chichicastenango and Antigua) is important to students of the Book of Mormon. Some BYU researchers have compared the area with the Book of Mormon and have come to the theory that Lake Atitlán could be the Waters of Mormon.

Pre-Columbian Mayan ruins are abundant in the country, especially in the highlands. Very few of them have been uncovered but the ones that have been excavated have manifested a magnificent culture.

Guatemala City itself was once the site of one of the largest and most progressive areas in Mesoamerica, long before as well as during the Christian era. Known as Kaminaljuyú, these partly excavated ruins can be seen north of the city. According to some Book of Mormon researchers, this could be the Land of Nephi.

Kaminaljuyú (Kah-me-NAL-hoo-YOO)

On the outskirts of Guatemala City lie some of the most interesting ruins of earlier times. It might be a good idea to ask at the tour desk of a major hotel or a tour guide the best way to reach the site.

The construction of the city of Kamilaljuyú was begun approximately 850 B.C. It continued to grow, until, by the Early Classic period, it may have been one of the largest of all the urban centers of its time with as many as 50,000 inhabitants. Several surrounding mounds, indicating buildings underneath, dot the landscape of this

Kaminaljuyú

fertile valley. Many groups lived here with each successive culture building over the previous one. Over 200 mounds have been counted.

The main temple has a single stairway leading to each stage, at the top of which is a temple sanctuary, roofed either with thatch or flat beam and mortar construction. The absence of stone sculpture is evident. There is evidence that prominent people of the community were buried inside the temple buildings. The temple platforms seem to have been built to enclose the rulers' tomb, with successive burials being placed over the older ones. Rich offerings of jade, pearls, mica, and textiles surround the bodies of the dead with more than one body usually found in the same area. The ceramics and jade date from 2000 to 1500 B.C., perhaps the oldest-known ruin in Central America.

Excavations allow the visitor to walk through narrow passageways to view some of the interiors by candlelight.

Kaminaljuyú means "Hills of the Dead People." This large religious metropolis influenced the growth of villages and lesser ceremonial centers.

Government leadership seems to have changed hands many times throughout the history of Kaminaljuyú. Examples of Izapa and Teotihuacán influence are quite evident at different times in its development. This suggests that at one time it may have been conquered by either one or both of these civilizations. The people of Kaminaljuyú traded with their neighboring cities and villages, and their influence and culture spread to other areas.

The people of Kaminaljuyú were skilled craftsmen who displayed their talents in the making of ceramics, jade, wood carvings, stone mosaics, and pottery. Gifted writers, they compiled almanacs and codices and decorated them with pictures from their religious lore.

The religion was dedicated to a number of gods: rain gods and little squat gods, but no Quetzatcoatl. Human sacrifice appears to have been practiced by removal of the heart from a living person.

Tikal (Tee-KAWL)

One of the most famous and photographed ruins of Mesoamerica, Tikal is synonymous with Guatemala. This pre-Columbian ruin is located close to the borders of Belize to the east and Mexico to the north. The best way to reach it is by flying from Guatemala City of Mérida, Mexico, and landing on an airstrip near the center of the Tikal ruin complex. Archaeologists from the University of Pennsylvania have been developing this area for a number of years.

Using current dating methods, these ruins date from approximately 600 B.C. which means that some of the structures are 2500 years old.

A visitor at Tikal will find this tropical area to be humid, warm and—depending upon the time of year—usually rainy. Sometimes monkeys can be seen swinging through the trees. Many colorful and graceful varieties of bird exist here, including the parrot and the heron. Beyond the ruins live the jaguar, puma, and ocelot as well as small deer and some snakes. The jungle is made up of zapote, logwood, mahogany, Spanish cedars, ceibas, sapodilla, and many low and high palms. All of these are interspersed with dense jungle vegetation.

The ruins are at the center of a 222-square-mile national park where a museum houses many of the artifacts found there.

An official expedition was made into Tikal in 1848, although it has been suspected that Spanish missionaries previously ventured into this general area. Modern studies of Tikal commenced with the work of Sylvanus G. Morley whose main concern was Mayan writing.

There are over 3,000 separate structures in Tikal. Included are temples, palaces, shrines, sacrificial altars, ceremonial platforms, residences, ball courts, terraces, causeways, bathing places and more than 200 stone monuments. Over 100,000 tools, ceremonial

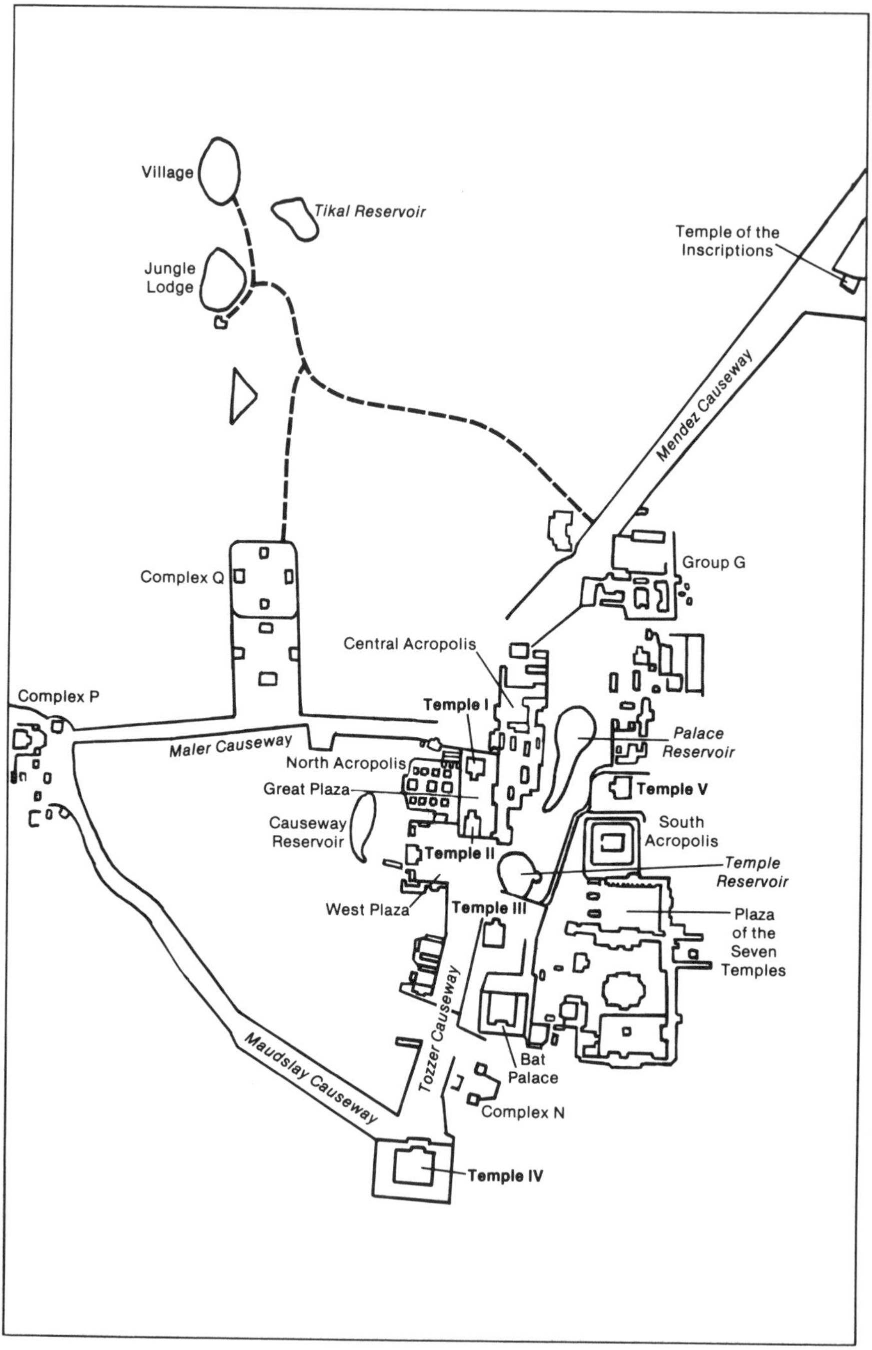
Village
Tikal Reservoir
Jungle Lodge
Temple of the Inscriptions
Mendez Causeway
Complex Q
Group G
Central Acropolis
Complex P
Temple I
Palace Reservoir
Maler Causeway
North Acropolis
Great Plaza
Temple V
Causeway Reservoir
South Acropolis
Temple II
Temple Reservoir
West Plaza
Temple III
Plaza of the Seven Temples
Tozzer Causeway
Bat Palace
Maudslay Causeway
Complex N
Temple IV

Tikal

objects, personal ornaments, and other items have been unearthed. Absent are the uses of gold and other metals, but beautiful jade jewelry and stone tools have been found. There are no underground rivers or wells like the cenotes in Yucatán. More than a million potsherds have been collected in this area. Almost without exception it was found that the existing structures were built over previous construction. In some places there is evidence that there were more than one or two underlying structures.

The age of the buildings at Tikal is a fascinating study. Some scholars conclude that a Pre-Classic period began at Tikal circa 600 B.C., a Classic period at A.D. 250, and a late Classic period at A.D. 550. This last period would include the collapse of Tikal about A.D. 900. Most of the buildings at Tikal (about 80 percent of them) were erected between A.D. 720 and 771. It is supposed that the entire 145 feet of Temple I was built in less than two years because the glyph date at the top is only two years later than the glyph date at the bottom.

The ruins are divided into nine major groups called "complexes" which are built around the Great Plaza. One of these complexes alone (Complex E) is built on a giant man-made platform ranging from 30 to 80 feet in height depending on the irregularities in the earth's surface. It is 650 feet by 500 feet in length and took at least 6,000,000 cubic feet of fill to build! But where did the fill come from? Possibly it came from the thirteen large reservoirs the people of Tikal built to supply their water needs. One of these alone holds 10,000,000 gallons of water.

The most magnificent structure still standing in this grand acropolis has been designated as Temple I, or Temple of the Giant Jaguar. This limestone building, 145 feet above the Great Plaza and built about A.D. 700, has nine sloping terraces and three rooms set behind each other in tandem fashion. It appears that the temple was painted in cream, red, and other colors, perhaps green and blue.

The temple chambers were spanned by high corbelled vaults, and Tikal is famous for its superb, fantastically carved wooden lintels. Inside, the towering Temple I consists of solid construction and is thought to be younger than Temple II.

Both temples appear to have been used for religious ceremonies and astronomical pursuits of the priests. Structure 39 is another interesting and somewhat unusual edifice. It is a large, oblong and unroofed room. Drains in the wall along the base seem to indicate that it was never intended to have a roof. An even more interesting structure is located near Temple III: structure 16. It is perfectly round and dated A.D. 711. It is made of crystalline limestone. The only known deposit of crystalline limestone capable of producing

Temple I, Tikal

Temple II, Tikal

Mayan Corbelled Archway leading to sacrificial center, Tikal.

Stone Stela 16, Tikal

Altar 5, Tikal

the amounts necessary for the construction of a building this size is located in the Languin Caves, 125 miles away.

Near the ruins are large carved monoliths (called "stelae") and sacrificial altars. The inscriptions on these stelae were not meant to be permanent because many of the carved stones were purposely destroyed by the Classic Mayas, and they were careful to smash the faces of the individuals depicted.

A causeway connects nearly all the temple complexes. The original was actually an eight-lane highway at least two miles long. In constructing it, a stone roadbed was laid then paved with a two-inch layer of lime mortar. Today it remains a solid road and would need only to be cleared to be used.

In the northern part of the main plaza are the remains of as many as 100 buildings with some buried over several earlier structures, one atop the other, and with the earliest dating back to 600 B.C.

Quirigua (CREEK-wah)

About 200 kilometers from Guatemala City on the way to the Caribbean Sea is the beautifully restored archaeological zone of Quirigua. The road to the area takes off to the right off Highway CA 9, the cross-country highway, and is easily seen. The ruin is of the same time period and style as Copan, Honduras, 30 miles north. The date of the first stele erected at Quirigua is A.D. 70, and the last is A.D. 810, indicating that the city prospered most during these times. These dates correlate with Book of Mormon era so the two civilizations were active at the same time.

It was rediscovered in modern times by John L. Stephens and Frederick Catherwood in 1840. Since that time it has been visited often. In 1901 the United Fruit Company bought the area and set aside the thirty acres surrounding the ruins as an archaeological site. In 1910 Sylvanus G. Morley and Egart L. Hewett began the excavation and restoration of two of the buildings. In 1914 the United Fruit Company hired E. H. Morris and Gustav Stromsvik to reconstruct the city's monuments. For years the only approach to the city was a footpath running parallel to the railroad tracks. Now, however, a road has been built which terminates at the ruins.

Quirigua's ceremonial center is quite small and seems even smaller than it really is because, at present, only the Great Plaza has been kept cleared of the jungle's encroachment. There are, however, many paths which cut through the jungle to the various excavated foundations. Many stelae and zoomorphs have been uprighted and

Carved Stele in Quirigua

25-foot Stele, Quirigua

Stylized Jaguar covered with hieroglyphic writing, Quirigua

restored at Quirigua including the largest known stela ever found at a Mayan site. This stele weighs 65 tons, is 35 feet from top to bottom, with 9 feet of it underground. The stele is one single piece of stone and is completely covered withintricate carvings. The quarry from which it was probably taken is three miles away. It must have been quite an engineering feat to transport a stone of this size.

Being as close to Copán as it is (thirty miles) and functioning at the same time, the two cities must certainly have had contact and an exchange of ideas. This seems to be borne out by the subject matter of the stelae which is the same at both sites. However, the variety at Quirigua is not quite as great as it is at Copán. Another difference is that monuments at Quirigua were erected at the end of every five years instead of the more common ten to twenty-year intervals. The first of these monuments were stelae which were continually more detailed and of greater splendor until Stele E—the enormous stone shaft—was erected; then ten years later, the erecting of zoomorphs at Quirigua began and very few stelae were erected after that. However, the customary five-year building of monuments continued with zoomorphs instead of stelae. The function of these zoomorphs was to commemorate important religious or social happenings within the society.

The ceremonial center at Quirigua is essentially divided into three groups which are centered around plazas, the temple plaza being the central—and apparently the most important—of these. The reason for this supposition is that the temple plaza is the only one which is surrounded by large temple or palace buildings. Northwest of the temple plaza lies another plaza. It is defined by arms extended out on three sides and with a small pyramid as the fourth side. There are no traces, however, of a building on top of the pyramid and it is, therefore, assumed to have been a ceremonial platform rather than a substructure for a temple. It has also been suggested that it may have been a convenient ampitheatre for watching ceremonies that took place in the plaza below. A mural depicting a pyramid being used for this purpose has been found at Bonampak.

East of this plaza lies the main plaza. It is the largest of the plazas and it is bordered on three sides with the fourth or west side left open. This is not uncommon in many ruins and can be seen at many sites.

There are also smaller groups of mounds which lie in the near vicinity of the main ceremonial center, but many of these have never been excavated nor even cleared of the dense jungle brush which has covered them for centuries.

Chichicastenango (Chi-chi-kass-te-NAIN-go)

A trip to Guatemala is not complete without a visit to Chichicastenango in the Guatemalan highlands where the most interesting open-air marketplace in the western hemisphere is found. This quaint Quiche (kee-chay) Indian village is located approximately 145 kilometers (two-and-one-half hours) west of Guatemala City on a road that leads off Highway CA 1. Since it is one of the most popular tourist attractions in the country, there are tours from the city that go to the village every market day—Thursdays and Sundays—but it is an easy drive if you have your own transportation. A large recreational vehicle would not be advised, however.

This is an opportunity to see a remarkable example of Indian life just as it has been for centuries. The market is for the Indians, not for the tourists. You can, however, buy anything there and many of the articles are obviously geared to appeal to the tourist trade.

On the market days the road is filled with Indian families coming from villages high in the mountains and carrying incredible loads on their heads and backs. They wear garments in bold hot pinks, magentas, blues, purples, and greens. The Indians sell their wares in front of the church of Santo Tomas where fervent religious ceremonies are an important part of the day. A strange combination of pagan and Catholic rites, these ceremonies consist of the traditional ritual of burning and offering a type of incense called "Pon," while the worshipers climb the steps to the entrance on their knees. After entering the church they light the candles on the floor and sprinkle different colored flower petals all around the candle bed.

Market Day in Chichicastenango

With Catholic priests walking around, the "curandero," or witch doctor, will perform his services on the floor inside the church also. The people buy small candles, the curandero places them on the floor, lights them, and chants for the people's problems, whether it be for crops or to rid themselves of a drinking problem. When alcohol is the problem, the curandero pours the tequila or whiskey on the floor of the church as part of his ceremony. Outside the church on the front steps is a large brazier where the curandero performs his service, using an abundance of great billowing, smoking incense. Later during the day some of them visit a nearby hill called "Pascual Abaj" to speak to the ancient stone idol. On a visit to Chichicastenango during the special holidays, the tourist will see the amazing "dance of the masks"—colorful, alive, and vibrant.

Chichicastenango is important because it is the place where the Quiche Maya wrote their book, *The Popol Vuh, The Sacred Book of the Ancient Quiche Maya.* After the conquest, under the direction of Catholic priests the Quiche Maya wrote a collection of the legends, traditions and histories of their people that had been passed down through the generations. As with the Bible, the *Popol Vuh* contains the story of the sea parting miraculously to allow fugitive tribes passage; both tell of a confusion of tongues and a tower of Babel; and both relate how sacred law was handed down to priests on a mountain top, the Maya god Tohil giving it to his priest, Chi-Pixab, just as Jehovah gave the law to Moses. The deluge story is also found in both books.

The original manuscript was written in the Quiche language in the characters of the Latin script. Father Ximénez, a parish priest of the village of Santo Tomas, Chichicastenango, translated the Quiche into Spanish.

The book is valuable because of its source and authenticity. One can see why the people in the New World so readily accepted the religion brought by the Spaniards. The Christianity taught by the Catholic priests was so similar to their ancient beliefs that the two religions dovetailed easily.

The Quiche Indian culture parallels in time with the Book of Mormon peoples. Both were flourishing during the early Christian era.

San Francisco

Scattered throughout the country and jungle areas of southern Guatemala are places of worship without benefit of building or churches of any type. Large carved stone heads are the center of this outdoor worship, and the native Indians gather before them in groups or they worship singly.

The service consists primarily in the placing of candles in front of the stone head. Incense, in the form of cedar chips placed in cans, is dangled on the end of two or three pieces of string. After lighting the incense, the person swings it back and forth while he moves around the stone, praying quietly. This procedure can last from several minutes to over an hour. While the father is doing this, any sons who accompany him stand by with folded hands and assist him when he beckons. Members of the family of the patriarch usually stay at home and maintain reverent silence until he returns.

Stone Face Worship, San Francisco, Guatemala

The Indians say that, although they are Christians and believe in Jesus Christ, they pay homage to these stone images to honor great spiritual leaders who lived prior to the time of Christ.

To see some of these heads, take Highway CA 1 to the little village of San Francisco. It is located between Chichicastenango and Huehuetenango (Whey-whey-te-NANG-go). Some of the heads are in shops in the town, but to see the larger head pictured, go out of town into the jungle. You will have to ask directions from the townspeople.

Zaculeu (Sah-koo-LAY-oo)

Zaculeu, which means "white earth," is located on a plateau in the Guatemalan Highlands close to the city of Hueheutenango, off Highway CA 1, in the shadow of the Chuchumatanes Mountains. The city is surrounded by barrancas and the area covered by the central part of the city is only three and one-third acres. Once an important ceremonial center, it was built sometime in the late Classic period (A.D. 550 to A.D. 900). Some Mayas were still living there at the time of the Spanish conquest.

Although Zaculeu is a Mayan city, it is nevertheless quite different from the lowland Mayan cities. One of the biggest differences between the lowland and the highland cultures is their architectural development. Scattered throughout the lowland sites, and yet entirely lacking in the highland culture, are the high, vaulted roofs and their intricate roof combs. In the highland culture, the temple roofs were wood-framed and rested on low columns which could not have supported heavy roof combs. Another obvious difference is the lack of ornamentation or sculptural elements in the highlands and the heavy use of it in the lowlands. At Zaculeu the buildings have only smooth surfaces. Also lacking are carved stelae and hieroglyphic inscriptions.

Between February 1946 and April 1949, a number of ancient buildings were restored at Zaculeu by the United Fruit Company and the Guatemalan government's Institute of Anthropology and History. This restoration at Zaculeu is one of the most complete of any ancient ruin in Guatemala. During the restoration it was discovered that nearly all the buildings were constructed with rough stone slabs which were cemented together with mortar after which a thick plaster coating was applied.

The city, which is dominated by a large, impressive temple, a ball court, and smaller buildings and temples, is completely surrounded by rivers, streams, trenches, and moats—its main type of defense.

Zaculeu's ceremonial importance is shown by its forty-three structures which are arranged in courts, or plazas. The largest temple was built in terrace fashion, with rough masonry walls covered with plaster, and with several sets of stairs leading to the top of the temple.

Many buildings in the city have three doorways and three rooms which some believe may represent the members of the deity.

The main portions of the buildings surrounding the ball court are raised platforms with stairs to enable spectators to easily reach their seats.

Temple Altar at Zaculeu

Central Plaza at Zaculeu

When excavated, the area revealed the foundations of long-removed altars with plain architecture and none of the ornate trimmings of Tikal. Zaculeu also was a burial ground; the graves housed not only the dead but such artifacts as beads, jade jewelry, bowls, jars, effigy pendants, figurines of all sizes and shapes, and pottery.

El Mirador

An exciting new chapter in the western hemisphere archaeology is being developed by a group of scientists in El Mirador, Guatemala. Dr. Ray Matheny, professor of anthropology and archaeology at Brigham Young University, is leading the excavations at the massive archaeological site begun in 1980. With Dr. Matheny as the project director, the team of archaeologists is endeavoring to learn more about the Maya who once occupied the massive site located in the Petén forest of Guatemala.

Archaeologists are becoming more and more convinced that El Mirador is the oldest and largest Maya city yet discovered.

Excavations began in 1979. Since then the site has attracted attention of professional and amateur alike throughout the world. The team is gradually chipping away at the jungle overgrowth to uncover new evidence that will add considerable dimension to the early Maya civilization developed in a massive area of the Petén which covers a large area of Guatemala and southeastern Mexico.

Deep in the Petén jungle, the site is located 120 kilometers (75 miles) from the frontier town of Flores, near Tikal. This is the major point of supply. Equipment and goods are flown from Flores to El Mirador in a Helio-Courier airplane. The trip takes about 35 minutes. The small village of Carmelita is about 60 kilometers (37 miles) south of El Mirador toward Flores. The road to Carmelita was open only one-and-one-half months in 1982 because of flooding. Normally, it is useable for two to two-and-one-half months each year.

A DC-3 flies to Carmelita two days each week to take services, then Carmelita provides mules and men for the trip to the project.

The crews are housed in tents, the field laboratory is a simple, thatched-roof hut, and the kitchen has a mud and rock stove. In a tropical forest, tenting is not particularly comfortable because of frequent rains and, usually, high humidity.

It takes sincere devotion for scientists to withstand these inconveniences, but they believe wholeheartedly in the project, and the scientists think the area will prove to be of great worth in the archaeological field.

Obviously, El Mirador is not a tourist site yet. But progress is being made all the time, so watch for later developments.

Copán, Honduras (Ko-pawn)

Copán is in Honduras a few miles from the Guatemalan border. It is thought to be the second largest ancient metropolis in the southern half of the Yucatán peninsula, and a great seat of learning for the ancient inhabitants.

There is a road leading off Highway CA 9 between Guatemala City and Quirigua; however, it is probably best to see this archaeological zone by plane from Guatemala City. Since Honduras is another country, crossing the border is involved. This often includes customs, papers, and regulations that are easier handled by a tour guide.

The main structure, covering about 75 acres, is composed of the Acropolis and five adjoining plazas. There are also sixteen subgroups which extend outward from this nucleus to a distance of seven miles. At the spectacular pyramids, terraces, and temples, some of the most complete inscriptions in Mayan hieroglyphics are found. The best example is a superb hieroglyphic stairway, 33 feet wide, with 62 steps, containing between 1500 and 2000 individual glyphs. Unfortunately, the stairway fell apart and the stairs ended up in a jumble at the bottom. It has been rebuilt, but since those who rebuilt were not able to read the glyphs, the stairs were replaced at random and hope of ever deciphering its message was lost.

Researchers believe that the important astronomical discovery of determining the exact length of intervals between eclipses was calibrated here at Copán, and that the great calculators and mathematicians regulated the peoples' lives by the movement of the heavenly bodies.

Elaborately carved altars and monoliths (stelae) found in the plaza represent the efforts of the greatest artistic sculptors of the time. But the elaborateness of these carvings was due to the nature of the ideas being expressed rather than from the desire to decorate every blank space with intricate design. Each element is an ideogram and presents a specific message.

Erosion from the river has exposed a vertical cross section 118 feet high and nearly 1000 feet long. Even earlier plaza floor levels and drains can be distinguished. Copán also claims the distinction of having the largest architectural cross section in the world.

Most of the monuments in Copán were built with 20-year intervals between their construction, and each building is dated. This ancient city is also the home of many burial tombs and markers carved with the Mayan hieroglyphics. The founding of Copán is placed at A.D. 176, according to the Mayan glyphs.

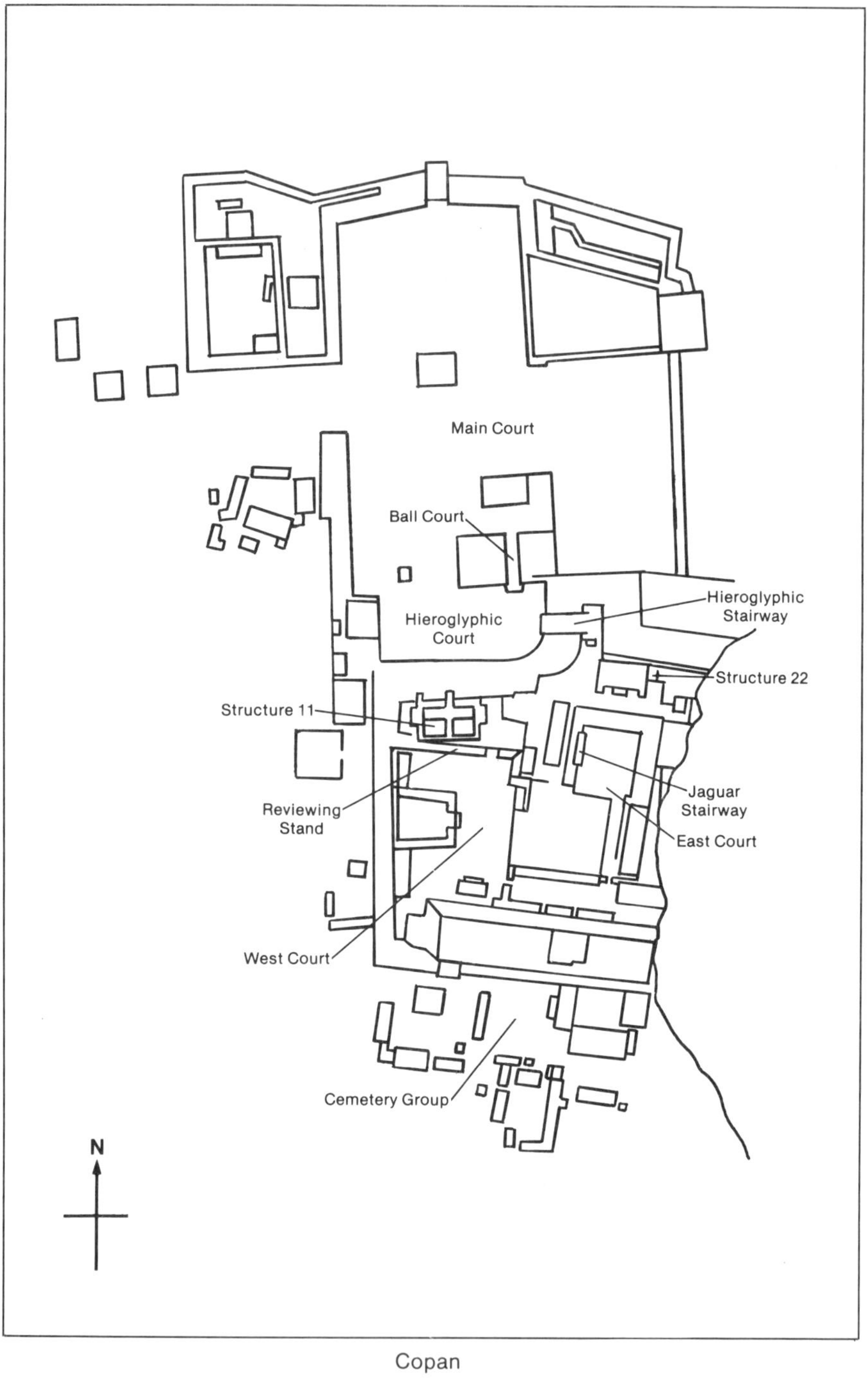
Main Court
Ball Court
Hieroglyphic Court
Hieroglyphic Stairway
Structure 22
Structure 11
Reviewing Stand
Jaguar Stairway
East Court
West Court
Cemetery Group
N

Copan

Stelae at Copán

Stela with Altar, Copán

Pyramid at Copán

Ball Court at Copán

CHAPTER FIVE

Tips for Traveling in Mesoamerica

Travel south of the border is a delightful adventure. Just outside your back door, you can journey into a "foreign" country. Differences in language and culture make it an enchanting and unique place to visit.

Mexico is a country of great contrasts—economically and geographically. Lean-to shacks or grass huts are common in villages, while palatial haciendas abound in the cities. Miles and miles of sagebrush and cactus give way to tropical jungle and snowcapped volcanic mountains. Seacoasts on both east and west are delightful playgrounds. Cancun and the Caribbean are a great competition for Acapulco and the Mexican Riviera on the shores of the Pacific Ocean.

The Paperwork

Requirements for entering Mexico are very simple. Tourist cards are required of all U.S. and Canadian citizens visiting Mexico for less than 180 days. Proof of citizenship (birth certificate, passport—always good to have—notarized affidavit, or voter's registration slip) is needed to obtain the free card. Canadians must have a valid passport.

Entrance into Belize, Guatemala, and Honduras is also easy, and usually can be taken care of at the border. However, it would be a good idea to consult the consulates of the countries to see what the latest requirements are for entry and vehicles. Mexican insurance is not valid in other countries, but coverage can be obtained at an agency at the Mexican border to the country.

Many people take their motor homes or trailers to Mexico. Areas all along the waterfronts have large settlements of trailer parks for the Americans and Canadians who are seeking the warmth of Mexican winters. In almost every town of any size along the main highways there are decent trailer parks or at least a safe place to park for the night.

Automobile and other vehicle permits are required for entry into Mexico. They are good for six months and may be obtained free of charge from the customs office at the border. Proof of ownership such as a license registration, a "pink slip" or legal title, or a notarized bill of sale is required to obtain this permit. You must keep your copy of the permit with your tourist card at all times and turn it in at the border when you leave Mexico.

Automobiles or auto accessories may not be sold while in Mexico, and you may not leave without your card except by making special arrangements for storing it under bond.

If the vehicle you are driving is not yours, you will need a notarized statement from the owner noting that you have permission to take the car into Mexico.

Your valid U.S. or Canadian driver's license is also valid in Mexico, but your insurance is not. Mexican insurance company agents at the border issue short-term policies at daily rates that are standard on either side of the border.

The Dan Sanborn Insurance Company can take care of all the requirements for entering Mexico, and they also furnish the traveler a mile-by-mile log of his trip. Tell the agent exactly where you wish to go and he will make up a personalized guide book that has explanations of sights along the road, maps, directions, a list of the restaurant, hotel, and trailer park accommodations in every town, and many travel tips. It is almost impossible for the book to be kept immediately up-to-date, but it is very close and the guide is invaluable. Sanborn Agencies are at every border town.

Driving in Mexico

To avoid trouble, obey the laws and follow the rules. Automobile accidents in Mexico are handled from a criminal rather than a civil standpoint. This means that drivers are liable to jail sentences in cases where fatal injury results, and even in minor accidents drivers may be held pending proof of innocence. Because of this arrangement, it is very important that you take out insurance coverage with a Mexican company. Policemen carry screwdrivers, and when an accident happens a policeman takes the license plates off the vehicles to insure that no one decides to leave the scene. When the fine is paid, the license is returned.

Unfortunately, if an accident occurs between a Mexican and a tourist, the tourist will probably be required to pay all expenses and fines regardless of who is at fault. An uncooperative attitude could land the tourist in jail where he is guilty until proven innocent. Keep a few pesos handy because, in a case like this, a "gratuity" can smooth the way out of a sticky situation. Don't let this culture trait make you apprehensive, though. Consider it an on-the-spot fine. Driving carefully and obeying the laws are extremely important.

One way to avoid trouble is *not* to drive at night. It can be hazardous to your health. The roads are narrow, the drivers only use parking lights until they absolutely have to turn on the headlights, and there are animals and slow-moving vehicles on the road with no lights on at all. As Sanborn says, "Burros don't have taillights."

Roads

Generally, the roads in Mexico are good, well marked, and they are being improved all the time. Areas accessible only by jeep a couple of years ago can now be reached by paved roads in ordinary cars. For this reason, it is important to get the most up-to-date map available. Near the large cities, such as Mexico City, the highways are divided and are as good as any in northern America. The average road, however, is two-lane with hardly any shoulder.

On the outskirts of towns, or anywhere speed should be reduced, there are "topes"—asphalt rises or bumps—in the road. These are very effective in controlling speed.

Traffic rules are not always obeyed by everyone else, so it is necessary to be alert, in no hurry, and to keep a sense of humor. Old buses and trucks never die in Mexico—they just keep plodding along. Carts pulled by one-donkey power have as much right-of-way as your 100-horsepower Detroit bomb.

The Mexican government is aware that tourists may need help along the highways, so they have the "Green Angels" patrol the roads. These are green, radio-controlled trucks run by mechanics who offer assistance when needed in the form of minor auto repairs, first aid, gasoline, towing, or tourist information. You will see the "Green Angels" all over Mexico, cruising around to find someone in distress. The service is free except for gas, oil, or parts.

When driving in Mexico, the "navigator" is as important as the "pilot." The driver has all he can do to watch other traffic and the road, so he needs someone to read the map and watch for road signs. Fixing snacks and drinks may also be part of the navigator's duties.

Mechanics in Mexico, even in the little places, are very good, so don't feel hesitant about having your vehicle repaired if it needs it. You should take along some simple tools and spare parts, especially if your vehicle is foreign-made or requires parts that are difficult to find. Good tires, including the spare, are very important to have. Don't be afraid to buy Mexican tires, though. They are good.

Gasoline

If you have a diesel-powered vehicle, your vacation to Mexico can be very inexpensive, especially if you have a recreational vehicle with its own bed and kitchen. Diesel fuel is much cheaper than gasoline.

Gasoline is plentiful in the many government-owned Pemex stations. The price is the same everywhere, and it is sold in liters (litros). One liter equals about one quart. There are two octane ratings—Nova (regular) in the blue pumps, and Extra (lead-free) in the silver pumps. The red pump has the diesel for all those trucks on the road. The Nova is very low octane. It will ping, and it can be harmful to new cars. However, the quality seems to be improving. It can be used in older cars if you retard the spark. Even though it costs more, the Extra is advisable and is recommended for high compression engines. Unfortunately, it is not available in many stations. If you have to buy Nova, buy only enough to get to the next town where Extra may be available. Nova does not ping at high altitudes as it does at low levels.

U.S. credit cards are not accepted at Pemex stations in Mexico, so be prepared to pay in pesos. Don't leave the car while the tank is being filled, and don't let the attendants work on both ends of your car at the same time. Keep them away from the motor until the gas tank has been filled. Check to see that you have your full measure and make sure the cap is on when the job is done. Then you can go to the restroom (Damas for her, Cabelleros for him).

When traveling in Mexico, the tourist soon learns to always have Kleenex and Wash 'n' Dries handy. Mexican public bathrooms are one of the things one has to learn to grin and bear.

Water

Like many other things in Mexico, water is improving. There is really no need for anyone to get the Turista, Montezuma's Revenge, or whatever you want to call the bug. Anyone who drinks or eats from the sidewalk vendors is asking for trouble, but the good restaurants and hotels are no problem because they use bottled water and ice made from purified water. It is advisable to stay in the best hotels and eat in the best restaurants you can afford to avoid spending your vacation feeling sick. If you do succumb, go to the "Farmacia" and ask for "medicina" for "diarrhea."

The best way to assure good water at all times is to use a Bondel or other kind of water filter. One model of the Bondel is a portable thermos-like filter, and contaminated water is cleaned in a minute.

When traveling in a recreational vehicle, a unit can be attached to the waterline under the sink, providing clean water at all times. This takes away all the worry about the water problem.

Another way to purify water quickly is to put a drop or two of bleach (Clorox, Purex) in a glass of water and let it set for a minute. Carrying a dropper-bottle of bleach can be very helpful in an emergency. The taste is not too bad if you don't put too much bleach in the water. This is really unnecessary in Mexico, as long as you are not in the backwoods.

Remember, the ice is usually not made from perfectly clean water, so be careful where it is used. The good hotels catering to tourists have clean ice.

Food

There is no need to carry large amounts of food with you unless your diet requires unusual things such as low calorie or low sodium. You might want to take along your favorite foods and drinks, just in case you can't find them in Mexico; however, in the larger towns there are "supermercados" that have everything, including many U.S. brands. In Mexico City and the western part of the country there are the Gigante (he-gahn-te) markets that equal any general-grocery store in the United States. In the eastern half of Mexico they are called Conasuper markets. These can be anything from the little corner store to a huge K-Mart-type plus a grocery department.

One of the fun things to do in Mexico is to shop in the native open markets or "mercado," whether in the cities or in Indian villages. Colorful and interesting, these markets provide the social outlet for natives. Since they have no refrigeration, the people have to shop every day. In areas where there are Indian villages, the people come to the market dressed in their native costumes which are always bright and colorful. Don't let them see you take their pictures, though. It is against their religion to be photographed, and it will make them angry. To respect others' feelings on such matters is only common courtesy. A few pesos will sometimes gain you permission to take the picture.

Beware of pickpockets in the crowded mercados and on narrow streets and sidewalks.

Fruits and vegetables are plentiful in Mexico, and are delicious because they are vine-ripened. Anything that can be peeled is safe. Bananas are especially good because they are not picked as green as those for shipping. Ripe ones are a good natural medicine for diarrhea, too.

Many of their vegetables are the same as those shipped to American markets. Tomatoes are safe to eat without peeling; pineapple and melons are really good, and sweet, too.

Health laws for meat are practically non-existent, as you will see in the open markets. Packaged ground meat purchased in the Gigante market presents no problem, but never buy any from the mercado vendors. Packaged luncheon meats and cheeses are good.

Browsing around the markets, whether Gigante or the Indian village open market, is a good way to absorb part of the culture. Take time to enjoy this pleasure.

Shopping

When buying souvenirs from vendors and tourist shops, bargaining is expected. A pretty good rule-of-thumb is to offer half the asking price. The salesman will plead poverty and give a pitiful tale of woe, but he wants to make a sale, so any reasonable offer will not be turned down. The price you pay will depend upon how badly you want it. If the item is just what you want and you turn it down with the hope of finding it cheaper somewhere else, you may be sorry. Many products are sold countrywide, but each area has its specialties that are not found elsewhere.

In the shops in the nice areas such as hotels, or city commercial areas (i.e. Zona Rosa—Pink Zone—in Mexico City) there is no bargaining and the price is set. The merchandise in these stores is usually of a very good quality. Typical souvenir items can be purchased much cheaper at the regular souvenir shops than at the exclusive ones.

Language

Knowledge of Spanish is helpful, obviously, but certainly not necessary in order to enjoy your trip to Mexico. You will naturally learn a great deal more about the country if you are able to converse with the people who live in it. You can get along surprisingly well with sign language, though, and it is almost always possible to find someone who speaks a little English. Most personnel involved in serving tourists speak good English, particularly in larger cities.

There are a number of inexpensive, pocket-size phrase books on the market that will give you the phonetic pronunciation of frequently used words. Many Spanish and English words are so similar that they are easily recognizable. For instance, a sign that says "Ruinas Arqueologico" obviously means "archaeological ruins." Some words in Spanish sound quite a bit alike, so it is important to pronounce them correctly. The word "camion" and "camaron" are good examples. "Camaron" means "shrimp," so when you go to a restaurant, make sure you pronounce it right, and not "camion" or you will get an order of trucks.

In Dan Sanborn's guide he tells of an easy way to ask directions. The word "a" (ah) in Spanish means "to." If you are not sure where you are going or whether you are on the right road, just stop and ask any Mexican, "Ah Veracruz?" or "Ah Motel Santa Fe?" or "Ah Mexico?" (that means Mexico City. Hardly anybody ever refers to Mexico City as Mexico City—they either call it just "Mexico" or "La Capital").

When you use "ah," by all means use a couple of gestures, too. With your forefinger, sort of point ahead down the road and at the same time nod your head in the general direction you are going. If you are on the right track, the Mexican will say "Si!" (yes), and you say, "Muchas gracias." If he says, "no" then turn around, head the other way, and ask somebody else, "Ah wherever you're going?" Sooner or later someone will say, "Si!"

If you have the opportunity, learn some Spanish. But don't let not knowing the language keep you from making the trip.

Medical Information

Take it easy for your first few days in Mexico, whether you fly or drive. It takes time to acclimatize yourself to the country, whether desert or mountain. Overindulgences in strange food, drinks and activities can reduce your ability to resist disease, and the infamous result is the so-called Montezuma's revenge.

There are plenty of pharmacies (farmacias) in Mexico, but it is a good principle to take along the basic items you will need to keep healthy and deal with your personal medical problems. Take copies of prescriptions you must have in case you mislay your supply. With regard to Montezuma's revenge, Kaomycin is frequently recommended as a cure; it has an antibiotic to kill the bacteria. Symptoms may be relieved by Kaopectate (Kaomycin without the antibiotic), Lomotil (anti-diarrhea), or paregoric (fights both diarrhea and stomach cramps, but is an opiate). Whether or not you take a drug, be sure to lie down and drink lots of fluids.

An alternative treatment is recommended by the U.S. Center for Disease Control (CDC). You'll need two clean glasses, a cup of fruit juice (eight ounces, about one-fourth of a liter), half a teaspoon of honey, a pinch of salt, a quarter teaspoon of baking soda and a cup of boiled or carbonated water. In one glass, mix the water and baking soda; in the other glass, mix the fruit juice, honey and salt. Sip from one glass, then the other. Believe it or not, this relieves diarrhea (as well as the dehydration). The CDC suggests that you not turn to antibiotics unless you have a high fever or blood in the stool, and does not recommend the old standby drugs—Lomotil and paregoric—for sufferers.

Many diseases that are uncommon further north are present in the subtropics and tropics, and you should consider protecting yourself against them. Before you go, renew your tetanus protection if necessary, and ask your physician whether you should have a typhoid booster shot. In Mexico, avoid going barefoot in areas where many people walk barefoot; some foot infections are common in parts of Mexico. Take along a good insect repellent and use it, because many diseases are carried by mosquitos and other insects.

A good sunscreen lotion is important. Hikers should also take an ace bandage, gauze bandages, and adhesive tape.

If you need a doctor, ask your hotel for a list of English-speaking physicians (or dentists) in the area. Any hotel catering to foreign travelers will have such information.

Weather and Clothing

The climate throughout Mexico varies more according to altitude than according to the season. The coastal areas and low sections of Yucatán and the interior are usually very warm, though there are occasional cool days in coastal areas during winter months. The climate is temperate at altitudes of 3,000 to 6,000 feet, and the cool zone extends upward from 7,000.

Mexico City is 7,400 feet high so weather is cooler there, and dress is more sophisticated.

The rainy season in Mexico is generally from May to October. Rains usually occur late in the afternoon and do not greatly inconvenience the tourist. Though the rainy season may not be the most popular tourist season, the countryside is at its greenest during that time, and many people prefer it to the dry winter months. Rain is possible in the "dry" season, too, so a rain hat, umbrella, and / or a light raincoat should be part of your wardrobe any time.

Layered clothing is always best for traveling. It can be quite cold nearer the U.S. border in the winter months, especially if it is stormy. The farther south you go the warmer it gets, but nights are chilly. You will be glad to have a jacket and a sweater, and to be able to peel down for the hotter weather.

Generally, dress is very casual and comfortable. Rubber-soled shoes are best for climbing around the ruins. A sun hat and sunglasses will help you be more comfortable in the Yucatán.

Photography

A tourist can be recognized anywhere by the camera around his neck. Taking pictures and reminiscing over them when you get home is one of the joys of traveling. Buy your film at home. It is much cheaper than in Mexico. It is best to have them developed at home, too.

When photographing throughout Mexico, remember you are a guest. Respect the Mexicans' privacy and beliefs; they are a proud and sensitive people.

Pets

Dogs and other pets may be taken into Mexico. Very few hotels will allow them, but most motels will. You must present a veterinarian's certificate stating that your pets are in good health. Rodent poison is often placed in seaport rooms, so check carefully before letting pets roam.

You will need a certificate, issued by a veterinarian and visaed by a Mexican consul, certifying that the animal has been inoculated for rabies within the last six months. If your pet is out of the U.S. for more than 30 days, you will need inoculation certificates to reenter the U.S.

Guns and Fishing Tackle

Any kind of firearms are illegal in Mexico, and you are asking for trouble if you take any across the border. For further information, check with your nearest Mexican consulate regarding gun permits and regulations.

Any reasonable amount of fishing tackle may be taken into Mexico duty free. You may pick up fishing licenses at the border or from local fish and game wardens. A fishing license is good in any state in Mexico.

Electric Current

You can take any electrical appliances you want to Mexico, because the current is the same as northern America.

When going by motor home, one has all the comforts of home, even to the television (many movies are in English with Spanish subtitles). If you travel by car, and don't like to eat all meals in restaurants, take along a little coil plug. When you stop at the motel at night you can have a cup of instant soup, cocoa, herb tea, or even boil eggs for tuna sandwiches. It would be just as easy to take along a fry pan or other small electric appliances and really cook a meal, if one wanted. Watch for hotel rules, though. Take an extension cord.

Evenings

Since it is not safe to drive at night (or even at dusk) in Mexico, plans must be made ahead to reach a landing place by sundown. You should stay there until sunup the next morning. In winter this makes for short driving days and long evenings, but it is necessary. Take books, games, or other pastime equipment. Many hotels do not have good lights for reading in bed, so you might want to take a small lamp and an extension cord. Electric outlets are scarce.

For entertainment, look in guide books or ask at your hotel.

Money

The Mexican dollar is a peso (pay-so), and it is divided into 100 cents (centavos). The peso sign is the same as our dollar sign, so it is easy to become confused. The rate of exchange varies so much lately that the only way to know what the dollar is worth is to check with the bank daily. There are many banks in Mexico.

Mexican money is strange to the tourist. You may think of it as "funny money" but it spends just like the American dollar. We wouldn't want foreigners to make fun of our money, so don't make wise-cracks in public about theirs.

It is almost impossible to cash a personal check there, so take plenty of small-denomination Travelers' Checks. The banks give the best rate of exchange. If you cash them in stores or restaurants, you can expect a lower rate. Hotels usually have the next best rate of exchange.

In tourist areas, the shopkeepers will be able to tell you what an item costs in American dollars, but when the visitor is away from the beaten path, he will have to figure it out for himself. Sanborn will give you a Mexican Currency Converter Card (it will be as up-to-date as possible), which is a great help.

You will not be able to use foreign money in Mexico, so stop at the bank at the border and change your dollars to pesos so you will have gas money for a while. Sanborn can change enough for you to get started, too. When you need more, go to a bank.

When you leave Mexico, cash in your pesos. Some of the Sanborn offices can help you there, too.

Most credit cards are accepted at hotels and the larger restaurants and stores. You will need pesos for gas, groceries, and souvenirs from the vendors.

CB's

The use of CB radios is now permissible in Mexico, and they are a tremendous help when two or more vehicles are traveling in a caravan. If you want further information about the use of the CB, check at the Mexican immigration station at your border crossing point.

The Sabbath

Even though there are many of them, the only way to find The Church of Jesus Christ of Latter-day Saints in Mexico is to know someone who knows where one is. Because of foreign ownership laws, the LDS Church (La Iglesia de Mormones) is not listed in telephone directories.

If you are able to locate one you will find the services in Spanish, of course. However, the same spirit is there and partaking of the sacrament in strange surroundings can be very comforting and beautiful. Even though you don't understand prayers given in Spanish you know the blessings on the bread and water are the same as in English.

To make Sabbaths more spiritual, you might find that you want to take along some of the many inspirational talks on cassette tapes that are great any time, and really while away the long stretches of road encountered at times.

If you do not have a built-in cassette player in your vehicle, a portable tape recorder does just as well. A power cord using the cigarette lighter plug gives unlimited hours of listening.

Guide Books

Since this book is not intended to be a complete guide to Mexico, you should find a guide book in a book store to use as a companion to this one. The professional guide books tell about each town and area as well as hotels, motels, restaurants, entertainment, and sightseeing. Trailer-park guides help those with recreational vehicles to find parks and facilities. To get the most out of your trip, these books are invaluable. The more you know of where you are going, the more you will enjoy your vacation.

Some Road Signs in Mexico and Their Translations

derecho	right
izquierda	left
peligro	danger
precaución	be careful
puente	bridge
conserve su distancia	don't tailgate
un solo carril	one lane
no rebase	no passing
cuota	toll
caseta de cobre	toll gate (get out your pesos)
despachio	slow
conceda cambio de luces	dim your lights
entrada y salida camiones	trucks entering and leaving road
no hay paso	do not enter
estacionmiento	parking
peligras máquinas trabajando	dangerous machines working
maneja con cortesia	drive with courtesy
ceda el paso	yield to right of way
carril izquierda	left lane
carril derecho	right land
carril izquierdo solo para rebarse	use left lane for passing only
transito lento carril derecho	slow traffic use right lane
desviacion	detour
parada	bus stop
aduana	inspection
alto (sometimes "pare")	stop
circulacion (on an arrow)	one way, yield right of way
preferencia (on an arrow)	one way, right of way
100 maxima	speed limit in kilometers

Just as in all countries, the shapes of signs have certain meanings. They are the same in Mexico and the U.S. (i.e., octagon for stop; triangle for yield; rectangle for speed limit, etc.). Pictures on the signs are very descriptive of their meaning, in many cases.

Name Pronunciations

Carocol	KAIR-ah-kall
Chac Mool	Chawk-MOOL
Chichén Itzá	Chee-CHAIN Ee-TSAH
Chetumal	Chay-tu-MAHL
Codz Pop	Kodes Pope
Copán	Ko-PAWN
Cuernavaca	Kwair-nah-VAH-kah
Cuicuilco	Kwee-KWEEL-ko
Dzibilchaltún	See-beel-chawl-TOON
El Castillo	El Caw-STEE-yo
El Tajín	El Taw-HEEN
Escarcega	Es-kar-SAY-hah
Huehuetenango	Whey-whey-tey-nang-go
Ixtlilxochitl	Eest-leel-so-CHEETL
Izapa	Ee-SAH-pah
Kabah	Kah-BAW
Kaminaljuyú	Kah-me-NAL-hoo-YOO
Kukulcan	Koo-kool-KAWN
Labna	LAWB-na
Mitla	MEET-la
Monte Albán	MOAN-tay Awl-BAWN
Oaxaca	Wah-HAH-kah
Olmec	Ole-mek
Palenque	Pah-LEN-kay
Petén	Pay-TEN
Puuc	Poo-ook
Quetzalcoatl	Kay-tsahl-KOH-ahtl
Quiche Maya	KEE-chay MAW-yah
Sahagun	Saw-hah-GOON
Tehuantepec	Tay-HWAN-tay-pek
Tenochtitlán	Tay-noche-teet-LAWN
Teotihuacán	Tay-o-tee-hwah-KAWN
Tikal	Tee-KAWL
Tlatelolco	Tlaw-tay-LOLE-ko
Totonac	Tow-tow-NAHK
Uxmal	OOS-mahl
Villahermosa	Vee-yah-air-MOE-sah
Xlapak	Slaw-PAHK
Xochicalco	So-chee-kall-ko
Xochimilco	So-chee-meel-ko
Yagul	Yaw-GOOL
Yucatán	Yoo-kay-TAWN
Zaculeu	Sah-koo-lay-oo
Zapotec	Sah-po-tek

Footnotes

1. *The Book of Mormon*, p. 364 (Helaman 3:7-11).
2. Kathleen M. Kenyon, *The Bible and Recent Archaeology*, 1978.
3. Friar Diego de Landa, *Yucatan Before and After the Conquest.*
4. Irene Nicholson, *Mexican and Central American Mythology*, 1967, p. 68.
5. *Ibid.*, p. 70.
6. Alma M. Reed, *The Ancient Past of Mexico*, 1966, p. 47.
7. Roman Pina Chan, *A Guide to Mexican Archaeology*, p. 52.
8. Adrian Garcia Valades, *Teotihuacán, The City and Its Monuments*, 1976, p. 9.
9. David A. Palmer, *In Search of Cumorah*, 1981, pp. 197, 199.
10. *Ibid.*, p. 204.
11. Bernal Diaz, *The Conquest of Mexico.*
12. *Ibid.*
13. Dr. Paul R. Cheesman, *The World of the Book of Mormon*, quote from "The Instructor," November 1968, p. 432.
14. Sylvanus G. Morley, *The Ancient Maya*, 1956, p. 294.
15. Victor W. von Hagen, *The Ancient Sun Kingdoms of the Americas,* 1961, p. 50.
16. *Op. Cit.*, Palmer, p. 170.

LDS Temple in Mexico City, Mexico. Courtesy of the Church News.

Index